Personality Disorders

T 70333

Titles in the Diseases and Disorders series include:

Personality Disorders

Hal Marcovitz

LUCENT BOOKS
A part of Gale, Cengage Learning

Detroit • New York • San Francisco • New Haven, Conn • Waterville, Maine • London

GALE
CENGAGE Learning™

LIBRARY OF CONGRESS CATALOGING-IN-PUBLICATION DATA

Marcovitz, Hal.
  Personality disorders / by Hal Marcovitz.
    p. cm. — (Diseases & disorders)
  Includes bibliographical references and index.
  ISBN 978-1-4205-0115-5 (hardcover)
1. Personality disorders—Juvenile literature. I. Title.
  RC554.M264 2009
  616.85'81—dc22
                                                            2008042290

Lucent Books
27500 Drake Rd.
Farmington Hills, MI 48331

ISBN-13: 978-1-4205-0115-5
ISBN-10: 1-4205-0115-1

Printed in the United States of America
2 3 4 5 6 7 12 11 10 09

Table of Contents

"The Most Difficult Puzzles Ever Devised"

Charles Best, one of the pioneers in the search for a cure for diabetes, once explained what it is about medical research that intrigued him so. "It's not just the gratification of knowing one is helping people," he confided, "although that probably is a more heroic and selfless motivation. Those feelings may enter in, but truly, what I find best is the feeling of going toe to toe with nature, of trying to solve the most difficult puzzles ever devised. The answers are there somewhere, those keys that will solve the puzzle and make the patient well. But how will those keys be found?"

Since the dawn of civilization, nothing has so puzzled people—and often frightened them, as well—as the onset of illness in a body or mind that had seemed healthy before. A seizure, the inability of a heart to pump, the sudden deterioration of muscle tone in a small child—being unable to reverse such conditions or even to understand why they occur was unspeakably frustrating to healers. Even before there were names for such conditions, even before they were understood at all, each was a reminder of how complex the human body was, and how vulnerable.

While our grappling with understanding diseases has been frustrating at times, it has also provided some of humankind's most heroic accomplishments. Alexander Fleming's accidental discovery in 1928 of a mold that could be turned into penicillin has resulted in the saving of untold millions of lives. The isolation of the enzyme insulin has reversed what was once a death sentence for anyone with diabetes. There have been great strides in combating conditions for which there is not yet a cure, too. Medicines can help AIDS patients live longer, diagnostic tools such as mammography and ultrasounds can help doctors find tumors while they are treatable, and laser surgery techniques have made the most intricate, minute operations routine.

This "toe-to-toe" competition with diseases and disorders is even more remarkable when seen in a historical continuum. An astonishing amount of progress has been made in a very short time. Just two hundred years ago, the existence of germs as a cause of some diseases was unknown. In fact, it was less than 150 years ago that a British surgeon named Joseph Lister had difficulty persuading his fellow doctors that washing their hands before delivering a baby might increase the chances of a healthy delivery (especially if they had just attended to a diseased patient)!

Each book in Lucent's Diseases and Disorders series explores a disease or disorder and the knowledge that has been accumulated (or discarded) by doctors through the years. Each book also examines the tools used for pinpointing a diagnosis, as well as the various means that are used to treat or cure a disease. Finally, new ideas are presented—techniques or medicines that may be on the horizon.

Frustration and disappointment are still part of medicine, for not every disease or condition can be cured or prevented. But the limitations of knowledge are being pushed outward constantly; the "most difficult puzzles ever devised" are finding challengers every day.

Personality Disorders: Widespread and Unpredictable

Just as fingerprints and DNA make each person unique, differences in personality make us who we are. But almost everybody knows someone whose differences get in the way of their relationships with others or their own happiness. Maybe that person takes offense too easily at an innocent joke. Maybe that person seems to talk about himself or herself too much or needs constant attention and praise. Maybe that person experiences wild mood swings, laughing hysterically one moment and showing a flash of anger the next. Maybe that person seems to enjoy hurting others. These are all behaviors associated with personality disorders that can have a devastating effect on the people who suffer from the disorders as well as the friends, family members, and coworkers who must live or work with them.

There are ten named personality disorders, each of which can range from mild to severe. Some involve a struggle with oneself; obsessive-compulsive personality disorder, for example, is often found among high achievers who strive, often too hard, for perfection. Some disorders involve a struggle against society; antisocial personality disorder, for instance, prompts many people to commit violent acts and other crimes. Among the better-known personality disorders are narcissistic personality disorder, whose sufferers need to feel important and in control but have no regard for the feelings of others; borderline personality disorder, which mental health professionals believe is responsible for many sui-

Personality disorders range from mild to severe and can seriously disrupt the lives of those afflicted, as well as those of their families and friends—and of society as a whole.

cides, particularly among teens; schizotypal personality disorder, which could prompt its sufferers to become delusional and unstuck from reality; and dependent personality disorder, in which a person becomes clingy, too reliant on others, and unable to make his or her own decisions.

Mental health professionals have concluded that personality disorders are responsible for a host of social ills. According to John Gunderson, director of personality disorders treatment at McLean Hospital in Belmont, Massachusetts, "The social costs of personality disorders are huge. These people are involved in so many of society's ills—divorce, child abuse, violence. The problem is tremendous."[1]

A Boss like Scrooge

Personality disorders are very common. According to the National Institute of Mental Health, some 9 percent of Americans—about 30 million people—suffer from personality disorders to some degree. Certainly, all personality disorders dominate the lives of the people who are afflicted with them, but they often affect other people's lives as well. Many criminals suffer from antisocial personality disorder; as they struggle with inner turmoil that often makes it difficult for them to tell right from wrong, they can inflict pain and suffering on innocent victims. In a marriage, if one spouse becomes too dependent on the other, a rocky relationship or divorce could result. In the workplace, the narcissistic boss or coworker can make it difficult for people to do their jobs, causing them to be unproductive or prompting them to look for employment elsewhere. In her description of narcissists in the workplace, nurse and author Mary Jo Fay points to Scrooge in Charles Dickens's *A Christmas Carol* as literature's quintessential narcissistic boss:

> The worst part of their behavior is that they do not see others as equal human beings: employees may as well be robots or machines as humans, for these narcissistic leaders do not comprehend that others have feelings, needs, and thoughts—the reason they are incapable of empathy or compassion in their dealings with "underlings." A vision of Scrooge comes to mind, constantly harping at Bob Cratchett to work longer, harder, and for less, and pouting like a child or having a temper tantrum when Bob asked to have Christmas Day off.[2]

Mental health experts have concluded that most personality disorders begin in early childhood. They believe a child's environment at home—whether he or she has loving parents or whether parents are cold, distant, or abusive—has a lot to do with how a child's personality is shaped.

Unpredictable Lives

What is common among most sufferers of personality disorders is the unpredictability of their lives. Indeed, people afflicted with antisocial personality disorder sometimes display intense flashes of anger, often accompanied by violent acts, for no apparent reason.

The lives of people with personality disorders are characterized by unpredictability and sometimes by outbursts of violent anger.

In 2008 twenty-four-year-old Christopher Gardner Beaman of Boston, a descendant of American statesman Henry Cabot Lodge, was charged with assaulting his girlfriend. Beaman's friends found the charges shocking. They knew Beaman to be a popular and friendly young man who often organized Frisbee matches and flag football games. But other witnesses at his trial told of a dark side: As far back as middle school, Beaman had assaulted other students, once breaking the arm of a girl on the school bus. While living in Colorado, he had compiled a long criminal record for assault, theft, and drug possession, and while undergoing psychiatric counseling, he was charged with assaulting his therapist.

In the 2008 case, Beaman was charged with punching his girlfriend so hard that he lacerated her liver. What shocked the victim was the suddenness of the attack: When Beaman approached her, she thought he was going to give her a hug goodbye; instead, he slugged her. After his arrest, prosecutors said he showed no remorse. "To think it's not important to you that you put someone in a wheelchair for a week tells me something,"[3] Judge Maurice R. Flynn told Beaman as he sentenced the defendant to a year in prison.

Beaman's attorney quickly provided the judge with an explanation for his client's conduct: Beaman suffers from antisocial personality disorder. "It came out of the blue," attorney Charles H. Riley told the judge. "Because of this rage disorder, this intermittent explosive disorder, he goes from zero to sixty."[4] Understanding the causes and effects of personality disorders is the first step in minimizing their costs to individuals and to society.

CHAPTER ONE

What Are Personality Disorders?

Some personality disorders are quite apparent. Mental health professionals would say that young people and others who have been in and out of trouble with the law for many years are clearly suffering from an antisocial personality disorder— they have no connection with the rules of society, they act on their own urges, and they are unable to control themselves. The person who seeks constant attention and applause from others, but disappears when things go wrong, is narcissistic. The girl who dresses provocatively, has extreme emotional outbursts, and constantly breaks up with boyfriends may have what is known as a histrionic personality disorder.

Somebody who purposely inflicts wounds on himself or herself, or attempts suicide, may suffer from a borderline personality disorder. "The most characteristic feature of the condition is multiple suicide attempts," says John Gunderson of McLean Hospital. "These attempts usually occur in the context of a problem in a relationship. These patients come into the emergency room, for example, after a fight with somebody, which leads them to take an overdose or slash their wrists."[5]

The traits that define other personality disorders are not as apparent or are not necessarily always negative. The quiet person who never seems to be involved with others, for example, may be more than just shy—he or she may be harboring an avoidant personality disorder. Some people have acknowledged their personality disorders and have learned to put certain traits to good use; for instance, many high achievers develop an obsessive-compulsive personality disorder, which helps them maintain order and direction as they excel in what can be very complicated jobs. Clearly, personality disorders manifest themselves in a wide range of traits and emotions, but the one unifying feature of all personality disorders is the tendency for them to make people act in ways that are strange and outside the range of what is considered normal, healthy behavior.

The *DSM-IV*

The ten named personality disorders are recognized by the American Psychiatric Association in the *Diagnostic and Statistical Manual of Mental Disorders (DSM)*, which was first published in 1952 and has undergone several revisions. The latest

People afflicted with borderline personality disorder may cut themselves intentionally or make repeated suicide attempts.

manual, commonly called the *DSM-IV*, serves as a guide for mental health professionals and helps them plan courses of treatment for their patients. According to the *DSM-IV*, a personality disorder is "an enduring pattern of inner experience and behavior that deviates markedly from the expectations of the individual's culture, is pervasive and inflexible, has an onset in adolescence or early adulthood, is stable over time, and leads to distress or impairment."[6]

The *DSM* did not recognize personality disorders as a unique category of mental illness until 1980; before then, it lumped some of the disorders in with other mental ailments. In each revision, the manual has refined the list of personality disorders—at one time listing as many as twenty-one separate disorders. In the *DSM-IV* the list is down to ten, grouped into three "clusters," according to the type of behavior exhibited by patients.

Cluster A: Odd or Eccentric Behaviors

Cluster A includes personality disorders in which people exhibit odd or eccentric behavior. Cluster A patients are also emotionally distant, distrustful, and suspicious. The Cluster A personality disorders are:

Schizotypal personality disorder. Schizotypals exhibit odd and eccentric habits, particularly in their manner of speech and dress. They harbor strange and outlandish ideas, many of which can be paranoid in nature, meaning that patients may suffer from intense and irrational fears. Also, schizotypals suffer from extreme anxiety in social settings and have difficulty forming relationships. They tend to talk to themselves and may be unresponsive during normal conversations with others. Some people with schizotypal personalities believe they have extrasensory perception, thinking they can see into the future and read other people's minds.

Boston psychiatrist Ronald Pies recalls that one of his schizotypal patients believed she was clairvoyant and claimed to have had foreknowledge of the 1986 mishap that resulted in the destruction of the space shuttle *Challenger*, which took the lives of seven astronauts. Says Pies, "I received a tearful call from my patient: 'It's my fault, Dr. Pies,' she said, sobbing into

Schizotypals and Creativity

People who suffer from schizotypal personality disorder may also be creative thinkers, according to a 2004 study performed at Vanderbilt University in Nashville, Tennessee. Researchers gave tests on creativity to people who have been diagnosed with schizophrenia and schizotypal personality disorder as well as a group of volunteers who do not suffer from either disorder.

During the tests, the researchers monitored the blood flow in the participants' brains and concluded that there was increased activity in the parts of the brains of schizotypals and schizophrenics where creative thinking and other highly cognitive processes take place.

The tests also indicated that the schizotypals use more of their brains to provide creative solutions to problems. "Their brains may be hard-wired for better creative thinking," says Vanderbilt researcher Brad Folley. In the test, schizophrenic patients were also found to be much more creative than the volunteers who do not suffer from the mental illness. Researchers speculated that there may be a genetic link between creativity and schizotypal personality disorder and schizophrenia.

Quoted in Anna Gosline, "Creative Spark Can Come from Schizophrenia," *New Scientist*, July 24, 2004, p. 14.

the phone. 'I had a feeling the shuttle was going to blow up, but I didn't warn anybody! I could have saved those people!' Much of our work together involved helping my patient feel less responsible for the misfortunes that befell others."[7]

One schizotypal patient of note is John W. Hinckley Jr., the Colorado man who attempted to assassinate President Ronald Reagan in 1981. Hinckley's shots, fired as the president departed from a Washington hotel after giving a speech, wounded Reagan as well as his press secretary, a policeman, and a Secret Service agent. Later, when Hinckley was evaluated by psychiatrists, they determined that he was schizotypal. He had become obsessed with the actress Jodie Foster and had concocted the scheme to kill the president to impress her. Hinckley was found not guilty by reason of insanity and has remained institutionalized since the assassination attempt.

Schizoid personality disorder. Schizoid personalities are introverted, withdrawn, and solitary people. They are cold to others and maintain distant relationships. They fear intimacy and closeness with others. They are absorbed by their own thoughts. They daydream a lot, but they do not often carry out their plans. "People with a schizoid personality are indifferent to normal social considerations and what others think of them," says Thomas Stuttaford, a British physician, newspaper columnist, and host of a television show that probes mental health issues. "They are emotionally restricted and happy to exist without close relationships. They do not display great anger or joy, are indifferent to praise and are cold and aloof."[8]

Schizoid and schizotypal disorders share some of the symptoms (as well as a similarity in name) with the mental illness known as schizophrenia, but mental health experts regard schizophrenia as a far different type of affliction. Schizophrenia is a mental illness in which the patient has an impaired vision of reality, often harboring bizarre delusions. It is common for schizophrenia patients to suffer from hallucinations. "Schizoids are lone wolves," says Norman Clemens, a professor of psychology at Case Western Reserve University in Cleveland, Ohio. "Schizotypals skate along the edge of real schizophrenia."[9]

Paranoid personality disorder. Paranoids misinterpret what others say, believing people treat them in a threatening or demeaning way. They do not trust others and are very suspicious of other people's intentions. They do not forgive others. They are prone to angry outbursts without reason. They perceive others as unfaithful, disloyal, condescending, or deceitful. They are jealous, secretive, guarded, and scheming. They are cold to others and often take themselves and others too seriously.

New York psychologist Alan Hilfer once found himself confronted by a neighbor who was diagnosed with paranoid personality disorder. The man, who lived in the apartment below, claimed Hilfer had stolen from him by breaking into his apartment. In retaliation, the neighbor attempted to leak gas into Hilfer's apartment, broke the windows of his car, verbally harassed Hilfer, and once threatened his twelve-year-old son. "He was convinced we had stolen his goods and even posed as an FBI [Federal Bureau of Investigation] agent to get 'the goods' on us,"[10] says Hilfer.

Cluster B: Dramatic and Emotional Behaviors

Unlike patients in Cluster A, Cluster B patients do not often lapse into delusional thinking. In Cluster B, patients often exhibit dramatic and emotional behaviors, usually sparked for reasons that others may regard as trivial. "Patients in this cluster can be among the most challenging patients encountered in clinical settings," says Randy K. Ward, an assistant professor of psychiatry at the Medical College of Wisconsin. "They can be excessively demanding, manipulative [and] emotionally unstable."[11] The personality disorders in Cluster B include:

Antisocial personality disorder. People with antisocial personality disorder—these patients are also known as sociopaths—ignore manners and other rules of social behavior, acting on their own urges and inner conflicts. They are impulsive, irresponsible, and have no regard for the feelings of others; nor do they show remorse for how they treat people. They act belligerently, aggressively, and violently, and they often have a criminal record because they may have been arrested for their conduct. They get bored easily and often turn to drugs and alcohol to ease their boredom and tension.

Antisocial personality disorder may be one of the most familiar forms of personality disorder because it is usually discussed in the newspapers after defendants are charged with violent crimes. Eric Harris and Dylan Klebold, the two teenagers who murdered twelve students and a teacher at Columbine High School in Colorado in 1999 before taking their own lives, are both believed to have suffered from antisocial personality disorder. After the tragedy, investigators found videotapes in which Klebold and Harris boast of their plans to launch an armed siege

Cluster B patients are characterized by manipulative behavior and emotional instability.

on their high school. "What's frightening is how cold and calculated all this was, with no regard for the consequences," says University of Iowa psychiatrist Donald Black. "They view it through their perverse world view, not seeing it as others would, which is a characteristic of antisocials."[12]

Borderline personality disorder. Borderlines maintain unstable relationships with others and often have a poor self-image. They are subject to wild mood swings. They are unpredictable and self-destructive, often turning to suicide attempts or self-mutilation to call attention to themselves. They view the world in extremes, regarding others as "all good" or "all bad." They fear abandonment and are excessively dependent on others, but they will often break off relationships quickly because of perceived slights. They are impulsive, chronically bored, and often respond with anger at inappropriate times.

Borderline personality disorder often afflicts teenage girls. Some girls say they start cutting themselves as an emotional release after breaking up with their boyfriends or when they find themselves under stress for other reasons. "I would do it when things got me upset," a seventeen-year-old girl named Brittany told *Time* magazine in 2005. "At the time, it was a relief, until you wake up the next morning, look at your arms and think . . . 'What did I do?'"[13]

The disorder was named in 1938 by psychotherapist Adolph Stern, who found that people who suffer from the disorder are on the borderline between psychosis, a major mental illness in which the patient loses contact with reality, and neurosis, a milder mental illness in which the patient feels stress but is still able to think rationally.

Narcissistic personality disorder. Narcissists have an exaggerated sense of self-importance and seek constant attention. They respond poorly to failure. They suffer from extreme mood swings and are exploitive of others. "Malignant narcissists are everywhere," says Pamela Kulbarsh, a nurse and crisis intervention specialist in San Diego, California. She explains:

Narcissists are exceptionally self-involved and display a constant need for attention.

You can find them in law enforcement, politics, business, the clergy, medical professionals, and in post offices. . . . Malignant narcissists seek omnipotence and total control, and will attempt to achieve those goals by any means. They will defy those in authority, challenge them, and attempt to demean them. Narcissists cast themselves as victims, justifying all their feelings and actions. They blame all of their shortcomings on perceived enemies.[14]

The disorder draws its name from Narcissus, the figure from Greek mythology who was seduced by his own reflection.

Histrionic personality disorder. Histrionics are extremely emotional and seek attention from others, but they are also sensitive to the approval of others. They may wear sexually provocative clothing and act in a provocative manner. They have an excessive concern over their physical appearance. They seek closeness with others, but they find it hard to share intimacy. Yet they make themselves believe they have intimate relationships with others. They experience wild mood swings, often featuring bickering and loud and ugly tantrums, but unlike borderlines, they are rarely self-destructive.

Perhaps history's most famous histrionic was General George Armstrong Custer, who won acclaim as a military leader in the Civil War but, years later, led two hundred cavalry soldiers into a disastrous attack on an overwhelming force of Sioux warriors, which ended in the massacre of Custer's troops at the Battle of the Little Bighorn. As a youth, Custer was impulsive, a show-off, and a prankster. As an officer, he favored flamboyant uniforms. His emotional outbursts and cravings for attention may have prompted him to order the attack on the Sioux. "He didn't just develop a flamboyant personality, it was part of his psyche," says Maryland physician Philip A. Mackowiak, who has studied the mental disorders of famous people. "And maybe that's what you had to be to be a successful cavalry officer."[15]

Cluster C: Anxious and Fearful Behaviors

The behavior of patients in Clusters A and B often become well known to others, either through their histrionic ravings, com-

Impetuous, flamboyant, and emotional, General George Armstrong Custer displayed the classic traits of histrionic personality disorder.

mission of crimes, suicide attempts, or paranoid and delu-sional accusations. In Cluster C, the symptoms tend to be more subtle and can often be missed or confused for other mental health issues, even by professionals.

People who fit into Cluster C typically exhibit anxious and fearful behavior. "All patients in this cluster exhibit anxiety in some form," says Randy K. Ward. "Whether it is caused by fears of evaluation by others, abandonment, or loss of order, these patients experience uncomfortable ideas and sensations that cause distress and interfere with their functioning."[16] The personality disorders in Cluster C include:

Obsessive-compulsive personality disorder. Obsessive-compulsives are extremely conscientious. They set high goals for themselves and strive for perfection, but they are never satisfied with their achievements and constantly take on more responsibilities. They are reliable, orderly, and methodical, but they are also inflexible, which makes it difficult for them to adapt to changing circumstances. They are extremely cautious and will weigh all aspects of a problem before proceeding, but they pay too much attention to detail, which makes it difficult for them to make decisions and complete tasks.

When events spiral out of their control and they find themselves relying on others, obsessive-compulsives often feel isolated and helpless. Certainly, obsessive-compulsive behavior can get in the way of a person's ability to maintain relationships and generally enjoy life, but many obsessive-compulsives have put the quirky symptoms of their personality disorder to good use. Noah Webster and Peter Roget, who spent their lives compiling lists of words and their de-

Capitalizing on his obsessive-compulsive traits, Peter Roget meticulously compiled comprehensive lists of synonyms and antonyms, which he published in his book *Roget's Thesaurus.*

finitions, were known to be obsessive-compulsive. Indeed, their personality disorder provided them with the patience to be excruciatingly careful and exact in selecting words and getting their definitions just right. Today, Webster's dictionary and Roget's thesaurus continue to be invaluable resources for the spellings, definitions, and usages of English words—both the products of obsessive labor by their authors. Roget began compiling lists of words at the age of eight and waited sixty-five years before he was confident enough in his work to publish his thesaurus. Moreover, he kept a careful log of his own daily activities, finally publishing his autobiography, which he titled *List of Principal Events.*

Obsessive-compulsive personality disorder should not be confused with obsessive-compulsive disorder, which is a far different mental health issue. Obsessive-compulsive disorder is an anxiety disorder in which the sufferer resorts to ridiculous and repetitive habits to confront his or her anxieties and fears. Somebody with obsessive-compulsive disorder may wash his or her hands constantly and repeatedly in response to an irrational fear of germs. "With obsessive-compulsive disorder, people become bombarded by very bothersome and intrusive thoughts," says University of California, Los Angeles, psychiatrist Jeffrey Schwartz. "Rather than providing them with pleasure or satisfaction, the obsessions impair their functioning."[17]

Dependent personality disorder. People who suffer from dependent personality disorder rely on others to make decisions for them. They are constantly seeking reassurance from others and are easily hurt by criticism. They do not like being alone and can be devastated if long-term relationships suddenly end. They lack self-confidence and usually do not initiate projects or act independently.

In a normal relationship, particularly one that involves spouses, it is normal for a husband and wife to depend on one another. Each spouse brings something to the relationship, and the partners soon learn to rely on each other's strengths and support one another in their weaknesses.

But the relationship becomes abnormal when one spouse becomes totally dependent on the other. "There are dependent people who panic easily, who are calling a friend or spouse fifteen times a day, undermining the relationship," says Robert F. Bornstein, a psychologist at Adelphi University in Garden City, New York. "These people may have dependency needs that are very intense."[18]

What often prompts the dependent member of the relationship to become clingy and panicky is an intense fear of losing the relationship. "This is the kind of couple where maybe the husband says, 'You're going to the store yourself? You're going to leave me here alone? You can't do that—here, I'll drive you,'" says Ronni Weinstein, a clinical social worker from Skokie, Illinois. "And this kind of trivial-sounding exchange can turn very demanding and even violent, because of this unreasonable fear of abandonment."[19]

Avoidant personality disorder. Sufferers of avoidant personality disorder are also very sensitive to rejection. They will not form relationships with others unless they are sure they will be liked. They are timid, fear criticism, and avoid activities with others. When they are in a group, they will remain quiet, fearing that what they say will be regarded as foolish. Outside of their families, they often do not have relationships with others and are troubled by their inability to relate to other people.

Shyness is a common trait shared by many people. Few young people have taken the stage for a school play or have stood in front of a class to give a presentation without feeling some degree of stage fright. But after a few nervous moments, most people are able to put their stage fright aside and function normally. Avoidants have a far more difficult time overcoming their shyness. "The patient with avoidant personality is essentially a shy, inhibited person who has feelings of inadequacy and low self-esteem,"[20] says Ward.

Avoidant personality disorder is believed to be similar to the mental illness known as social phobia. Like obsessive-compulsive disorder, social phobia is a reaction to an irrational fear. Social phobia manifests itself in a fear of other people and often a fear of leaving home, which is known as agoraphobia. People who suffer from social phobia do not go out much, they maintain few close

Crippled by timidity and low self-esteem, avoidants have difficulty forming relationships.

friends and are afraid of how others will perceive them.
Stuttaford, the British physician and newspaper columnist, says
avoidant personality disorder often affects patients much more
deeply than social phobia because social phobics know they have
a problem and often cry out for help, but avoidants seem willing
to accept their conditions. According to Stuttaford:

> The . . . specific condition that may give rise to an abnor-
> mal approach to other people is avoidant personality dis-
> order. The problem usually starts early in childhood, and
> is characterized by the same fear and humiliation and crit-
> icism of the social phobic, although much worse. As a re-
> sult, they have no friends, or perhaps only one, other than
> their close relatives. They not only fear humiliation but
> have a dread of any situation where they are going to be
> judged. Their life is very solitary, but unlike many socially
> phobic patients, their horror of other people and their
> judgment is so great they have accepted it without ques-
> tion.[21]

History's most famous avoidant was probably Greta Garbo,
the 1930s movie star who once uttered this line of dialogue in
a movie: "I want to be let alone." Evidently, Garbo was not acting—she really did want to be let alone. Garbo retired from the
movies while still relatively young, living out her life as a vir-
tual recluse.

Angry and Loving, Mean and Nice

While it may seem as though the *Diagnostic and Statistical
Manual of Mental Disorders* has done a very tidy job of classi-
fying the ten personality disorders, many mental health experts disagree. For starters, it is not unusual for some patients
to suffer from more than one personality disorder. Some psychiatrists and psychologists have suggested that more research
is needed on how multiple or mixed personality disorders affect patients' behaviors. Certainly, a patient who is both antisocial and paranoid may be a truly dangerous individual.

Moreover, mental health experts point out that the classifi-
cations do not differentiate patients who suffer from very mild

Dissociative Identity Disorder

Dissociative identity disorder is a rare mental illness in which the patient's personality splits into more than one identity. In many cases, the patient has no memory of what he or she may have done while assuming an alter ego. At one time, the condition was regarded as a personality disorder—in fact, it was known for many years as "multiple personality disorder"—but in 1994 psychiatrists changed the name after gaining more insight into the condition, and they recategorized it as a mental illness, not to be grouped with the ten named personality disorders in the *DSM-IV*. Patients with dissociative identity disorder, it is now believed, do not harbor more than one personality; rather, their single personality splits into numerous identities—they dissociate from their true identities.

The most famous case of dissociative identity disorder on record is that of Shirley Ardell Mason, a Minnesota woman whose story was dramatized in the 1973 book *Sybil*. (Her true name was protected by the book's author.) Mason had been sexually abused as a child and developed sixteen separate identities within her personality. In 2008 the former football star Herschel Walker published an autobiography, *Breaking Free*, in which he also claimed to suffer from dissociative identity disorder. Walker says he developed multiple identities to deal with anger and other turmoil in his life.

or very severe versions of the same personality disorder. Therefore, according to the manual, a patient exhibiting just a few mild symptoms of obsessive-compulsive personality disorder is grouped together with a patient whose obsessive-compulsive tendencies are controlling his or her life. Since the manual also recommends treatment guidelines for personality disorder patients, critics suggest that the categories should be further refined to reflect the differences within each disorder. As psychologist and author Jeffrey J. Magnavita explains, "Two patients diagnosed with an obsessive-compulsive personality disorder may be functioning at very different levels of adaptive functioning and thus treatment and prognosis might be very different."[22]

Still, psychologists and psychiatrists have spent decades studying personality disorders and have concluded that people who harbor these strange and troubling tendencies are truly in need of counseling and other therapies to help control behaviors that are often bizarre and harmful to themselves and others. University of Michigan psychologist Randolph Neese says, "Most of us are angry sometimes and loving sometimes, nice sometimes and mean sometimes. But people with personality disorders keep doing the same things over and over again. Their emotional palette isn't varied."[23]

CHAPTER TWO

What Causes Personality Disorders?

T he study of personality disorders is a relatively new science. Only within the past century have psychologists and psychiatrists started to explore why some people's personalities prompt them into eccentric, antisocial, and violent behaviors. Before mental health experts focused on what may go wrong in someone's personality, they spent many years defining personality and researching personality development.

They concluded that a personality is composed of the thoughts, feelings, and behaviors that make a person unique. Among mental health experts, there is some disagreement on how the personality develops and whether it can change throughout a person's life. Many mental health experts believe that a personality is formed very early in childhood and remains consistent for a person's entire life. In other words, they believe it is rare to find someone who for years was known as bright, cheerful, and outgoing but at some point turned dour, grumpy, and secretive. Other experts are not so sure; they suggest it is possible for personalities to constantly change, sometimes for the better, sometimes for the worse.

Regardless of how personalities form, mental health experts are largely in agreement about how they can go bad. Indeed, there are many reasons people develop personality disorders, including traumatic events in their childhoods, inherited traits from their parents and other family members, and poor environments at home and other places that have influenced how they view themselves and others.

The Surly Man

The study of personalities dates back to ancient Greece. In the year 280 B.C., the teacher and philosopher Theophrastus published a work titled *The Characters*, in which he describes thirty different personalities one was apt to meet on the streets of Athens. (Theophrastus was actually a botanist whose work identifying various types of plants would influence generations of scientists; nevertheless, *The Characters* proves he was also a keen observer of people and their eccentricities.) Theophrastus describes people prone to surliness, arrogance, boasting, and various other eccentric behaviors that today would fit neatly into the descriptions of personality disorders defined by the *Diagnostic and Statistical Manual of Mental Disorders*:

The Surly man is one who, when asked where so-and-so is, will say, "Don't bother me"; or, when spoken to, will not reply. If he has anything for sale, instead of informing the buyers at what price he is prepared to sell it, he will ask them what he is to get for it. Those who send him presents with their compliments at feast-tide are told that he "will not touch" their offerings. He cannot forgive a person who has besmirched him by accident, or pushed him, or trodden upon his

In 280 B.C., Greek philosopher Theophrastus described various human behaviors that today are labeled personality disorders.

foot. . . . When he stumbles in the street he is apt to swear at the stone. He will not endure to wait long for anyone; nor will he consent to sing, or to recite, or to dance. He is apt also not to pray to the gods.[24]

Theophrastus may not have known it, but in explaining the personality of the surly man he was describing elements of paranoid and antisocial personality disorders.

For two thousand years, surprisingly little was added to Theophrastus's observations. Then, in 1920, Sigmund Freud, the Austrian physician whose studies laid the groundwork for the science of modern psychiatry, addressed the development of personality by identifying three factors in the formation of personality: the id, ego, and superego. According to Freud, the ego drives a person's reactions to events in real life, while the superego serves as the conscience, pro-

In the 1920s, Austrian physician Sigmund Freud identified three components of personality, which he called the id, the ego, and the superego.

viding a moral compass. Freud believed the id exists in the subconscious, driving a person's thoughts and actions in ways in which he or she has no control. Freud believed a personality was like an iceberg; very little of it exists in plain sight, and most of a personality is hidden beneath the surface. According to Freud, the personality driven by the id is the part beneath the surface. Freud suggested that the id, ego, and superego are in constant conflict, which may explain why personality disorders often surface. Freud also believed that personality was established by the age of five.

As mental health experts learned more about how personalities develop, they conceived theories about why some people develop abnormal personalities. Psychiatrists and psychologists expanded on Freud's theories, with some believing that personality develops past childhood in stages, and that if things go wrong during one or more of the stages, personalities can develop bad traits such as antisocial or ruthless behavior. They also suggested that if children suffer through traumatic experiences early in life, such as the loss of a parent, they can fixate on their loss and carry it with them through the rest of their lives, a factor that would certainly affect the development of their personalities. Eventually, psychiatrists and psychologists also concluded that personality traits can be inherited, hardwired into people's DNA. They also speculated that environment can shape personality; specifically, that a child's personality can be largely influenced by the quality of life at home and what he or she observes in others, particularly parents and other family members.

Men and Women

Studies have also shown that men and women suffer from personality disorders in roughly equal numbers, but some personality disorders are more likely to afflict men, and others seem to mostly affect women. For example, some 75 percent of the sufferers of borderline personality disorder are women. Most people who harbor histrionic personality disorders are women. Antisocial personality disorder, in contrast, is far more common among men. As neurobiologist Debra Niehoff explains:

> People are not born bad. But being born male seems to be a step in a violent direction. . . . Antisocial personality disorder . . . is three times more common among men than women. Rapists, stalkers, and mass murderers are predominantly men. Serial sexual killers, the most feared violent criminals, are, as far as forensic experts can tell, exclusively men.[25]

Mental health experts believe the roles that women and men are assigned in society often promote personality disorders.

Bumps on the Head

For centuries, the study of personality made little progress. In 1809, however, an Austrian neuroscientist, Franz Joseph Gall, developed an outlandish theory that, nevertheless, gained a considerable measure of support within the scientific community. Gall suggested that the bumps he found on a person's head were important indicators of personality—a theory eventually named phrenology, after the Greek term for "study of the brain."

Gall divided the surface of the head into twenty-six regions representing various emotions, sentiments, feelings, and intellectual abilities. By performing a physical examination of the surface of the head, Gall believed, he could determine the size of each of these regions and, therefore, their influences on the patient's personality.

Phrenology was given a large measure of weight until better science eventually found other reasons why people act as they do. By the end of the nineteenth century, phrenology was thoroughly discredited. "Medicine gradually distanced itself from its mid-19th century phrenology frenzy," says Stanley M. Aronson, the former dean of Brown University Medical School. "Its loyal proponents were no longer physicians but now members of an eccentric cult; and a few charlatans who found a ready audience amongst the more credulous. Phrenology persists now in circus sideshows next to the lady who reads palms."

Stanley M. Aronson, "The Three Professional Roles of Dr. Gall," *Providence (RI) Journal*, January 24, 2000, p. B-7.

In 1809, Austrian neuroscientist Franz Joseph Gall developed the theory of phrenology, which was later discredited.

For example, in most cultures women have traditionally been taught to be submissive to men, a factor that could lead some women to develop dependent personality disorders. Men, on the other hand, are often taught to show strength by keeping their emotions bottled up. As Gayleen L. McCoy and William E. Snell Jr., the authors of a 2002 Southeast Missouri State University study on gender differences in personality disorders, explain:

> Antisocial personality disorder occurs more often in men than in women, because men, more so than women, are raised to think for themselves and to keep their feelings and emotions inside, which leads them to act without thinking about anybody but themselves. While growing up, men are taught to inhibit their affection or tenderness toward people and family, because such behavior would be considered feminine. So, if men, more so than women, are exhibiting inhibited affection, then it would seem to suggest that antisocial personality disorder and inhibited affection would be . . . associated with one another.[26]

Experts believe that the male tendency to hide emotions can contribute to the development of antisocial personality disorder.

On the other hand, some mental health experts believe that personality disorders form in generally equal numbers among men and women. They suggest that the diagnoses of borderline personality disorder in women have little to do with how the disorder affects the sexes but can instead be attributed to the inability of many psychiatrists and psychologists to properly diagnose their patients. According to Judy Gershon, a spokeswoman for the Borderline Personality Disorder Resource Center in White Plains, New York:

> While about 75 percent of those diagnosed with borderline personality disorder are women, it is believed there are many more men with it who have not been diagnosed properly. The character portrait of an individual (with borderline personality disorder) would be one who is caught in a storm of extreme emotional swings, in many instances leading to self-destructive and reckless behavior, such as substance abuse and self-mutilation.[27]

Roots in Childhood

While mental health experts debate the issue of how gender affects personalities, most are in agreement that personality disorders have their roots in childhood. The case of Gary Lee Sampson serves as a typical example. The Massachusetts man was convicted in 2003 of the murder of three men. According to prosecutors, Sampson chose his victims at random.

Throughout his life, Sampson had been diagnosed with borderline and antisocial personality disorders. Psychiatrists traced Sampson's troubles to an unhappy childhood. "He had a real mean streak growing up," said Abington, Massachusetts, deputy police chief David Majenski, who knew Sampson as a boy. "He had a propensity toward violent outbursts. He was certainly someone who lashed out at anyone who crossed him. He was a troubled youth. Police certainly knew who he was. He was someone that we knew growing up to stay away from."[28]

Witnesses testified that Sampson started using marijuana at the age of eight and cocaine and heroin at the age of thirteen. As a boy, they said, Sampson had been ridiculed in school by classmates

Erik Erikson

The psychotherapist given much of the credit for determining how personalities develop is Erik Erikson (1902–1994), a Danish immigrant who taught at Yale University School of Medicine in Connecticut and also served as a researcher at Yale's Institute of Human Relations. During his career, Erikson also worked in research at Harvard University and taught at the University of California.

Erikson was educated in Europe, where he was acquainted with Sigmund Freud. Freud believed people's personalities are formed by the age of five, but Erikson argued that personalities continue to develop in adults. However, he was steadfast in his belief that childhood represents an important moment in the development of a personality. "You see a child play," he once said, "and it is so close to seeing an artist paint, for in play a child says things without uttering a word. You can see how he solves his problems. You can also see what's wrong. Young children, especially, have enormous creativity, and whatever's in them rises to the surface in free play."

Erikson also studied personality disorders and suggested that the home, workplace, and other aspects of the environment have an impact on personality. He suggested that if people suffer trauma in their childhoods, they develop inner scars that they carry with them into adulthood.

Quoted in *New York Times*, "Erik Erikson, 91, Psychoanalyst Who Reshaped Views of Human Growth, Dies," May 13, 1994, p. B-9.

as well as teachers because he was a slow learner. Witnesses also said Sampson was physically abused by his father and a brother. "He said that his father told him that he was evil and horrible, and that he was no good," social worker Joan Katz testified during Sampson's trial. "He said it began at early childhood and never let up. It was a dreadful relationship."[29] As an adult, Sampson drifted from one relationship to another. First married at the age of seventeen, he was soon divorced and would go on to marry four more times. He also maintained homosexual relationships and attempted suicide more than once.

Having lived through such dark times as a child, psychiatrists were hardly surprised that Sampson turned to a life of crime as an adult. Before his arrest for the three murders, Sampson had compiled a long police record for numerous robberies and other violent acts. During Sampson's trial, psychiatrist Angela Hegarty testified, "He knew what he was doing was wrong, but he lacked the capacity to stop himself. He lacked the capacity to do what he knew was right."[30] Certainly, Sampson's poor self-image, his wild mood swings, and his self-destructive behavior such as drug use, prior suicide attempts, and multiple marriages, were all symptoms of a borderline personality. Essentially, he reacted to the stresses in his life by hurting others as well as himself. His total disregard for others and inability to stop himself from inflicting harm on other people pointed to an antisocial personality disorder. As for the jurors who decided Sampson's fate, they were unmoved by the evidence of his troubled childhood: They sentenced the defendant to the death penalty.

Nature or Nurture?

Sampson's troubled childhood is not unique among personality disorder patients. Studies show that some 70 percent of borderline women were sexually or physically abused as children. It is also common for narcissists to have suffered through abuse and trauma as children; these incidents lead to the low self-esteem and self-loathing that therapists believe is the source of narcissists' need for praise and attention. The high divorce rate in America may also reflect traumatic influences on early childhood development. Children who may not have been physically or sexually abused might have been traumatized through family conflict, loneliness, or the loss of a parent. Meanwhile, they may have had much less of a support system at home. Perhaps they not only grew up in one-parent households but also saw little of grandparents, aunts, and uncles who were thus not available to give them support. Says Larry Siever, a professor of psychiatry at Mount Sinai School of

Medicine in New York, "In the past, we lived close to our extended families in highly structured communities. People could take care of their own and rein them in."[31]

Gary Lee Sampson may have suffered through a troubled upbringing, but it is also possible that he was born with borderline personality disorder genetically wired into his brain. During the trial, Sampson's lawyer asked psychologist Thomas Deters, "Are you able to determine when Mr. Sampson's brain went bad?"[32] Deters responded, "Well, I think it started out bad."[33]

Indeed, recent studies have indicated that abnormal personalities can be inherited from ancestors, just as blue eyes and premature balding can be handed down from generation to generation. Psychiatrists and psychologists have long noted that histrionic personality disorder seems to run in families.

Antisocial personality disorder is also believed to be an inherited trait. A 1999 study by psychologists in Great Britain and Sweden looked at the lives of fifteen hundred pairs of twins and concluded that aggressive antisocial behavior was more common in identical twins than in fraternal twins. (Fraternal twins, who develop from separate eggs, are not as genetically linked as identical twins.) Another study of twins, conducted in 2000 by Norwegian psychologists, found that identical twins were likely to share personality disorders—in the study, 69 percent of the borderline personality disorder cases were found among identical twins. "There are almost certainly multiple genes involved in predisposing people to personality disorders,"[34] says John Gunderson of McLean Hospital.

The question of how much of an impact a child's home environment or genetic makeup has on his or her personality is one that has long been debated by mental health experts. Many psychologists and psychiatrists argue that it is often difficult to tell the difference between the two. They suggest that if a child is forced to grow up in an unloving home where he or she faces abuse, then it is likely the child's parents also suffer from personality disorders and, therefore, it is likely they have genetically passed their personality disorders on to their sons and daughters. "Will a gene ever be found for personality disorders?" asks psychologist Jeffrey J. Magnavita. "It is certain that

Convicted murderer Gary Lee Sampson is seen at a court hearing. Psychiatrists say that his antisocial and borderline personality disorders may have been inherited.

both nature and nurture influence personality, though the extent of the contribution of each remains unclear."[35]

Normal Events

Whether the child develops a personality disorder through an inherited gene or through experiences at home, it should be noted that not all personality disorders evolve from bad genes or troubled home environments. Even normal events in a child's life can affect his or her personality and lead to personality disorders. For example, Jeff Lewis grew up to be a successful California real estate investor. He had what can be regarded as an ordinary childhood and yet he is convinced that his obsessive-compulsive personality disorder has its roots in his youth. "If my parents didn't give me separate plates for my chicken, mashed potatoes, and spinach, I would get visibly anxious and wouldn't eat anything,"[36] he says.

Even the best and brightest young people are not immune to personality disorders. Some gifted children develop narcissistic personality disorders. Identified as gifted at early ages, they are often lavished with praise by their parents, teachers, and coaches, made to feel special simply because they were born with extraordinary intellectual or athletic talents. Such attention can often feed a young child's narcissism. Indeed, after years of being told they are gifted, they may develop narcissistic personalities as a way to deal with failure. As author and psychotherapist Alice Miller explains,

> Quite often we are faced here with gifted patients who have been praised and admired for their talents and their achievements. . . . According to prevailing general attitudes, these people—the pride of their parents—should have had a strong and stable sense of self-assurance. But exactly the opposite is the case. In everything they undertake they do well and often excellently; they are admired and envied; they are successful whenever they care to be—but all to no avail. Behind this lurks depression, the feeling of emptiness and self-alienation, and a sense that their life has no meaning. These dark feelings will come to

the fore as soon as the drug of grandiosity fails, as soon as they are not "on top," not definitely the "superstar," or whenever they get the feeling they failed to live up to some ideal image and measure they feel they must adhere to. Then they are plagued by anxiety or deep feelings of guilt and shame. What are the reasons for such narcissistic disturbances in these gifted people?[37]

Personality Changes in Adults

While much of the research into the development of personality disorders has focused on young children, some mental health experts argue that adults can also develop personality disorders. Adults who are the victims of significant head trauma, caused through traffic accidents, criminal acts, warfare, sports injuries, or similar reasons, can often recover physically from the surgery but be plagued by mental illness for the rest of their lives. In fact, a personality change in an adult stemming from severe brain trauma was first chronicled more than 150 years ago.

In 1847 a railroad worker named Phineas Gage was injured while blasting rock to lay tracks in Vermont. Gage was struck in the head by an iron bar, which pierced his skull like an arrow. Miraculously, he survived the accident as well as the operation to remove the iron bar, losing only the vision in his left eye, which had been pierced by the chunk of iron.

Still, after the accident Gage was a changed man. Before the accident, he was regarded as intelligent, shrewd, energetic, and well liked by others. After the accident, Gage became a man of little patience, quick to grow angry, cool to the opinions of others, unable to finish jobs, and a user of foul language. Obviously, Gage sustained significant brain damage during the accident, which affected his personality. He died in 1860.

Brain trauma is only one way in which the personalities of adults can develop disorders. In older adults, personality changes often become evident during the early stages of Alzheimer's disease. The disease usually afflicts patients who are in their seventies or older, although cases of Alzheimer's in

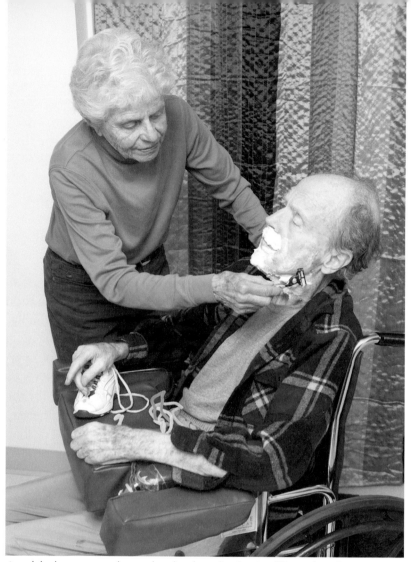

An elderly woman shaves her husband, who is afflicted with
Alzheimer's disease.

younger patients are not rare. Alzheimer's patients suffer from
severe memory loss—eventually, their memories almost com-
pletely escape them, and they have little recollection of events
in their lives, regardless of whether they occurred a few sec-
onds ago or several years in the past. They do not remember
the faces or names of their loved ones, friends, and others they
see day to day. Moreover, they forget how to brush their teeth,
bathe themselves, use the toilet, and perform other simple
tasks. Many live out their lives in nursing homes, where they
receive round-the-clock care.

An early warning sign of Alzheimer's is often a change in personality—the patient may become hostile or suspicious of other people, exhibiting symptoms of paranoid personality disorder. "Family members and caregivers of Alzheimer's patients often describe the alterations of personality that occurred during early stages of the disease," write authors and Alzheimer's disease experts Rosemary Snapp Kean, Kathleen M. Hoey, and Stephen L. Pinals. "Symptoms of apathy, irritability, poor energy, or agitation appear before any significant [memory loss] changes occur."[38]

Even younger adults can undergo personality changes. In 2003 psychologists at the University of California, Berkeley, released a study suggesting that people's personalities do change as they grow older. The study found some personality changes in adults as young as twenty-one. Indeed, the study found that as many people grow older, they start developing traits that are often found in personality disorders. For example, the study found that people tend to become less open or comfortable among others as they grow older—symptoms common among schizoids, paranoids, and avoidants. On the other hand, the study also found that as people grow older, they become less rash, more agreeable with others, and more stable in their relationships—indications that people who suffer from personality disorders may see their symptoms abate somewhat as they age.

Regardless of whether personalities continue to change as people grow older, there is no question that most personality disorders have their roots in how patients were treated as children. Were they physically or sexually abused? Did their parents treat them coldly? Did they learn how to be abusive by watching the ways in which older brothers or sisters treated others? Are they antisocial because they were born into a family of criminals whose law-breaking ways are hardwired in their genes? "It's likely that these childhood abuse factors do play an important role," says Tracie Shea, an associate professor of psychiatry at Brown University Medical School in Rhode Island. "It's hard to say how big that role is, more specifically."[39]

CHAPTER THREE

Living with Personality Disorders

The football player who prances defiantly after scoring a touchdown and then takes full credit for the team's success (and none of the blame for the team's failures) is one example of how the personality disorder of narcissism can affect some people. The antisocial student who disrupts class, bullies others, uses drugs and alcohol, and commits senseless vandalism is obviously affecting the lives of innocent people. The borderline teenage girl who responds to a breakup with her boyfriend by inflicting cuts or burns on herself is clearly suffering through her personality disorder, but it is also likely that the people who care about her are suffering through her troubles as well.

People afflicted with personality disorders have a very difficult time maintaining normal lives. Indeed, their lives are dominated by fear, anxiety, or reckless behavior. Certainly, if their personality disorders lead them into lawlessness, they will also have an impact on the lives of others, most likely the people they victimize.

In 1995 the case of Susan Smith made international headlines when the South Carolina woman was arrested for drowning her two young sons in a car that she drove into a lake. At her trial, psychotherapist Seymour Halleck testified that Smith suffers

Divas Should Calm Down for Their Own Good

Histrionic behavior is sometimes called diva behavior, named after the female opera stars who are talented yet arrogant, fussy, high-strung, and difficult to work with. Evidence suggests that diva behavior—the constant bickering, screaming, and throwing of tantrums—can be hazardous to the health of the diva as well as of the people forced to listen to the diva's tirades.

Histrionic fits can put stress on the body, raising the levels of the natural chemicals produced by the body, such as adrenaline and cortisol, which speed up the heart rate and interfere with digestion. (This may explain why many histrionics suffer from heartburn, a painful irritation of the esophagus.) "It's like having a wave of Drano [drain cleaner] go through your body," says New York psychologist Ellen McGrath.

Diva behavior can, of course, cause stress on the unfortunate people who find themselves on the receiving end of a histrionic fit. Soon, McGrath says, friends and family members will not take it any longer, and they stop listening. "The tolerance for these people wanes," says McGrath. "Like the boy who cried wolf, after a while [the divas] become hard to take seriously."

Quoted in Jennifer Magid, "Scene Stealers," *Psychology Today*, October 2007, p. 45.

from a dependent personality disorder. "[She] feels she can't do anything on her own," Halleck said. "She constantly needs affection and becomes terrified that she'll be left alone."[40] Halleck said Smith, abused as a child and clinically depressed for much of her life, maintained relationships with many men out of her morbid fear of being left alone. This fear, he said, led her to try to kill herself by driving her car into the lake. Smith escaped from the car at the last moment but did not try to save her children. Smith was eventually convicted of causing the deaths of her children and sentenced to life in prison.

Susan Smith, who was convicted of drowning her two sons, suffers from a dependent personality disorder.

Most people who suffer from personality disorders are able to control their emotions, far more successfully than Smith; nevertheless, chances are their personality disorders have had some impact on their lives as well as the lives of others.

Charges of Narcissism

In some cases, personality disorders can affect many more people than just close friends or family members. In 2005 when football star Terrell Owens engaged in a very public and very nasty spat with his team, the Philadelphia Eagles, the fallout affected the team's play on the field, the team's fans, and just about everybody else who followed the sport. Owens is a talented wide receiver who signed with the Eagles before the 2004 season. Owens turned out to be the missing piece of the puzzle for the Eagles, providing them with the one significant player they needed to get to the Super Bowl. Although the team came up short in the title game of the National Football League (NFL), the Eagles had great hopes for 2005. But the 2005 season turned into a disaster, as Owens grumbled in public about his contract, taunted his teammates, and alienated the fans. The Eagles had been a championship-caliber team in 2004, but in 2005 the team fell out of contention and compiled a losing record; clearly, the furor stirred by Owens in the locker room and elsewhere was largely responsible for the team's losing record. Owens became such a divisive figure that the Eagles took the unprecedented step of suspending him for the final four games of the season.

Professional athletes play in front of tens of thousands of spectators as well as millions of fans who watch on television. Many of them perform with a flare for showmanship, but throughout his career Owens has always seemed to find a way to call attention to himself. In 2000 he enraged Dallas Cowboys fans when, after scoring a touchdown, he posed defiantly on the team logo, a star painted at midfield. The brazen show of ego cost him a week's suspension. In 2002, after scoring a touchdown on a nationally televised *Monday Night Football* game, he produced a pen from his sock, autographed the football, and handed it to a friend in the stands. After the autograph incident, Owens said:

Some people in the NFL and the press called me an embarrassment to the sport, shameless, selfish, egotistical, and worse. . . . They don't want to see or hear anything that will make them think very much about the people who work for them. The press can't understand that when I went to the star in Dallas, I wasn't trying to taunt anyone but was thanking and honoring God for all the blessings I've received and for all the things I've been able to do for my family.[41]

When he arrived at the Eagles' training camp before the start of the 2005 season, Owens had already made it clear he intended to cause trouble. During camp, team officials sent him home to cool off—he responded by putting on a show of calisthenics in his driveway in front of a horde of fans and reporters. "I was just having some fun," Owens said later. "I wanted to show people that I wasn't crying and depressed. I wanted everybody to see me smiling and having a good time. The footage was everywhere on TV. All of America saw it."[42]

Throughout his dispute with the Eagles, Owens was forced to fend off charges that he is a narcissist. "As the worst of the narcissists in the NFL, Owens is incorrigible, addicted to acting up before the camera's eye, no matter how strained and pathetic it comes across,"[43] insisted *Washington Times* sports columnist Tom Knott. Dan Le Batard, a sports columnist for the *Miami Herald*, added, "T.O. [Terrell Owens] is a narcissist . . . bloated on so many of the adult things we dislike about his childish workplace, but at least his ego is there for all to see."[44]

A Pall over Baseball

Owens is not unique in professional sports. Another professional athlete whose actions have been regarded as narcissistic is Pete Rose, the disgraced baseball all-star who was found to be gambling on games while managing the Cincinnati Reds. As punishment, the baseball commissioner issued a lifetime ban, prohibiting Rose from ever working again in Major League Baseball, a fact that has kept him out of the sport's Hall of Fame. For nearly fifteen years, Rose denied gambling on baseball; finally, in

The performance and reputation of the Philadelphia Eagles pro football team suffered due to the narcissistic behavior of gifted player Terrell Owens, shown here playing for the San Francisco 49ers prior to joining the Eagles.

Baseball manager and all-star player Pete Rose's lifetime ban from Major League Baseball cast a pall over the sport.

a 2004 biography, he admitted to betting on games, including those in which he managed. Critics reacted harshly, suggesting that Rose admitted to gambling in a half-hearted gesture intended to show baseball officials that he is serious about rehabilitating himself. His critics suggested that Rose believes he is such a big star that once he owned up to his previous misdeeds baseball would welcome him back. "By all accounts, Rose has a huge ego. . . . He appears to believe baseball needs him as much

The Narcissist of North Korea

Kim Jong Il, the dictator of North Korea, has exhibited many per-sonality traits that suggest he is a narcissist. Kim, who stands five feet three inches (1.6m) tall, is very sensitive about his height but also vain about his appearance. He is known to wear platform shoes and comb his hair in a bouffant style so that he appears to be taller than he is. Diplomats who have encountered Kim have described him as warm, charming, and conversant, but behind the scenes the ruthless North Korean ruler is known to possess a quick temper, a lack of empathy for others, and no conscience.

The son of a former dictator of North Korea, Kim grew up in lux-ury but was very suspicious of his siblings and other family mem-bers, whom he suspected of plotting against him. According to George Washington University psychology professor Jerrold Post:

Unlike his father, Kim Jong Il grew up in luxurious surroundings, pampered, raised to be special. This is the formative recipe for a narcissistic personality, with a grandiose self-concept and diffi-culties with empathy—the characteristics he displays indicate that he has the core characteristics of the most dangerous per-sonality disorder, malignant narcissism.

Quoted in Jonathan Curiel, "Mad, Bad, and Very Cunning: The Puzzling Psyche of North Korea's Leader Is on Display," *San Francisco Chronicle*, July 23, 2006, p. E-1.

North Korean dictator Kim Jong Il is said to have a narcissistic personality.

as he needs it. He may believe he is bigger than the game," says New York psychologist Richard Lustberg. "Narcissists expect favorable treatment and that deludes [Rose] into believing baseball will eventually cave to his need."[45]

While Owens hurt himself by losing nearly $2.5 million in salary and bonus payments during his suspension, and Rose hurt himself by facing a lifetime ban from his sport, both athletes also hurt their organizations. Owens damaged the Eagles' chances of winning in 2005, and Rose's gambling habit cast a pall over Major League Baseball, suggesting that gamblers have influence over the outcome of games. Their narcissistic behavior affected their teammates, other players, and millions of fans. David Carter, director of the University of Southern California Sports Business Institute, says narcissists in sports are no different than narcissists in any organization or company. "By the time they've hung themselves, they've really gone a long way to impacting the morale of the rest of the organization and done a fine job of contaminating the company in the marketplace,"[46] he says.

Bill the Shark

The conduct of Rose and Owens had wide-ranging impacts on their teams and fans, but there is no question that the behavior of narcissists as well as others who suffer from personality disorders affects the lives of people closest to them. The selfishness of a narcissist will surely damage a marriage; a narcissist's spouse or children may turn to alcohol and drugs to relieve the stress of living with somebody with a personality disorder. Family members forced to live with histrionics must endure constant bickering, complaining, and tantrums. Annie Paul Murphy, author of *The Cult of Personality*, recalls the case of an attorney named Bill who, at the age of twenty-six, had already been married and divorced twice and whose antisocial behavior had touched several other lives as well:

> They call him "the Shark." Bill, a 26-year-old lawyer, is proud of his nickname and the ruthlessness that inspired it. Confident and charming, he can also be arrogant, manipulative and deceptive—though he sees nothing wrong

with these qualities, useful as they are in winning cases and attracting women. Lately, however, Bill's character has been landing him in trouble. He's begun abusing cocaine. He can't resist the temptations of strip clubs and casinos. He's already been married and divorced twice. Even his successful career has been endangered by his habit of propositioning female coworkers.

Bill is bothered enough that he pays a visit to a psychologist's office. There he's told that he has an "antisocial" personality: He consistently, and often unscrupulously, places his own interests above those of others.[47]

While friends and family members of narcissists must often endure verbal and psychological abuse, spouses and children of antisocials may also be abused physically. Even if they are not abused, family members of antisocials and others who suffer from personality disorders often are puzzled by the wild mood swings and odd behaviors of those afflicted, making it difficult to maintain relations with them.

Princess Diana, movie star Marilyn Monroe, and artist Vincent van Gogh all had difficulty maintaining relationships with the people who were closest to them. All three are believed to have suffered from personality disorders. All three craved attention and led self-destructive lives.

Diana is believed to have harbored a borderline personality disorder; she attempted suicide and suffered from eating disorders and self-mutilation. During her marriage to Prince Charles, Diana is believed to have slashed her chest and hurled herself into the glass door of a bookcase as she sought release from her mental anguish. She exhibited other symptoms of borderline personality disorder as well. She is said to have been suspicious of others, reacting to that impulse by eavesdropping at doors and opening other people's mail. She ended relationships quickly, often shedding friends for reasons that remained a mystery to the people who thought they were close to her. She was very dependent on others, though, and carried several cell phones with her so that she could constantly be in touch with friends.

Diana, Princess of Wales, pictured with her husband, Prince Charles, is said to have exhibited the traits of borderline personality disorder.

Indeed, just a few months after her marriage to Charles, Diana was already exhibiting wild and unpredictable behavior. Biographers have reported that she spent entire days weeping in silence, resisting efforts by friends to console her. She would slip out of the couple's opulent home at Kensington Palace in London, making anonymous phone calls to people she knew. Worried that the calls could be traced to her cell phone, Diana sometimes used a public phone booth. After her marriage to Charles ended, she maintained several romantic relationships. She is believed to have been very dependent on her final boyfriend, department store heir Dodi Al-Fayed, with whom she died in a 1997 car accident. One of her biographers, Sally Bedell Smith, concludes, "Diana's unstable temperament bore all the markings of one of the most elusive psychological disorders: borderline personality."[48]

Diana lived through an unhappy childhood, which can, of course, spark a personality disorder. Her parents, members of British aristocracy, were divorced in a venom-filled case that became very public, thanks to England's aggressive tabloid press. Another celebrity known to have an unhappy childhood was Marilyn Monroe. With a mentally ill mother and a father who abandoned the family, the future movie star grew up in a series of orphanages and foster homes. She was never able to maintain a stable relationship; Monroe was married and divorced three times and carried on many other brief but notorious romantic relationships. Mental health experts believe she may have been borderline and perhaps also dependent. Helpless, weak, clingy, and insecure, she died of a drug overdose in 1962 at the age of thirty-six. "Marilyn Monroe was probably borderline," suggests John Gunderson of McLean Hospital. "Her whole life was tempestuous and maybe more typical of a borderline patient's life. Even when they have done something creative, they are likely to be embedded in a very inconsistent record of productivity, as well as involved in many tumultuous relationships."[49]

The nineteenth-century Dutch painter Vincent van Gogh may also have been a borderline. His wild mood swings were well known by his friends. One of his close friends, the French artist Paul Gauguin, once fended off an attack by Van Gogh, who came at him with a razor blade. "He tended to form these rather exclusive relationships with one person and would become territorial, possessive, jealous about their time,"[50] says Gunderson. Indeed, Van Gogh's act of self-mutilation has been well documented in many biographies of the tragic and troubled artist: He cut off his own ear.

Van Gogh died in 1890. After spending his final years in and out of mental institutions, the artist took his own life. He was thirty-seven years old.

Managing Their Emotions

Diana, Monroe, and Van Gogh were famous people, but their symptoms are no different than those suffered by all people with personality disorders. Teenage girls are among the most common sufferers of borderline personality disorder and the most likely patients to mutilate themselves. "If a kid is repeatedly self-injuring, they need help," says New York psychiatrist Barbara Stanley. "What it says is they are having trouble managing their emotions. They have hit on this one area of managing their emotions and they find it works."[51]

Friends and family members who are searching for answers about why a teenage girl may exhibit such bizarre behavior need only look for scars on her wrists or other places on her body—the marks of self-mutilation are a sure sign of borderline personality disorder. Of course, other personality disorder patients also send out warning signals. The case of Shawn Woolley provides a typical example.

Woolley spent much of his time alone, rarely leaving his apartment except to work in a pizza restaurant. At home, he spent as much as twelve hours a day playing the online computer game EverQuest. The twenty-one-year-old Wisconsin man was totally consumed by the game, shunning relationships with others, living mostly in the EverQuest fantasy world. Woolley's family was concerned about his addiction to video games and urged him to seek counseling. A psychologist interviewed Woolley and concluded that he suffered from a schizoid personality disorder. Indeed, Woolley led a solitary life, withdrawn from others, lost in the fantasy world of a video game.

Woolley's mother, Elizabeth Woolley, recalls an incident that upset her son: Shawn had become despondent after an online competitor cheated at the game. "He was so upset, he was in tears," Elizabeth Woolley says. "He was so depressed, and I was trying to say, 'Shawn, it's only a game.'"[52]

In 2001 Woolley committed suicide, taking his own life with a gun while in the throes of his fantasy world. Indeed, evidence suggests that he had been playing the game just moments before pulling the trigger. Certainly, millions of young people play violent and action-packed video games every day. For the most part, they are able to separate the fantasy world of the game from their real-life world of school, homework, and family. But in Woolley's case, his schizoid personality disorder prevented him from maintaining normal and healthy relationships. David Walsh, president of the Minnesota-based National Institute on Media and the Family, says, "Could a person get so engrossed that they become so distressed and distraught that it could put them over the edge? It probably has something to do with the game. But your average person or average gamer wouldn't do this."[53]

Woolley's personality disorder led to self-destructive behavior and, ultimately, the loss of his own life. Steven D. Green's personality disorder led to the loss of life for innocent people. The former infantry soldier is charged with the rape and murder of a young Iraqi girl as well as the murders of three members of her family. Green has been diagnosed with antisocial personality disorder. The case has made international headlines, showing how a personality disorder can lead to a horrific outcome.

As with many personality disorder patients, Green suffered through a troubled childhood. His parents divorced when he was four; later, his mother was jailed for drunken driving. As a teenager, Green was also known to use alcohol. Making it only as far as the tenth grade, Green dropped out of school. In 2005, at the age of nineteen, Green was jailed on an underage drinking charge. Soon after his release, Green enlisted in the U.S. Army and, eventually, was sent to Iraq. While serving in Iraq, Green is alleged to have led five other soldiers to the home of the Iraqi family, where he committed the rape and murders. Green is facing the death penalty.

As Green faces trial, U.S. Army officials have been forced to reexamine their recruitment procedures to determine how somebody with an antisocial personality disorder—in other words, a psychological powder keg—slipped through their psychological screenings, was handed a gun, and was sent to a war zone. Experts believe that most soldiers with mental health problems are

While serving in Iraq, Steven D. Green—since diagnosed with antisocial personality disorder—led Jesse V. Spielman (pictured) and four other soldiers to an Iraqi home. There, Green allegedly raped a young girl and killed her and three other family members.

weeded out during basic training, known in the military as boot camp. Still, Green managed to slip through. "It isn't Army policy to retain somebody who isn't dependable," says Loren Thompson, a military analyst for the Lexington Institute, an organization based in Arlington, Virginia, that studies national security issues and other public policy matters. "I'm certain this person slipped through the cracks. . . . The whole point of boot camp is to find people who can't hold up under stress and get them out before they get in the field."[54]

Societal Ills

The Woolley and Green cases show how personality disorders can lead to destructive and even truly horrific consequences for those afflicted as well as for others. In contrast, there are many personality disorder patients whose behavior has few other consequences than simply being annoying to others. In New York, for example, twenty-year-old actor and children's bookstore employee David Andrejko admits to odd and eccentric behavior. Angry at how he was being treated by his employer, the histrionic staged a tantrum in the store, throwing himself into a display table, knocking over a toy train. "The other day I was so fed up with changes around the store that I tried to stage a walkout," he says. "Unfortunately, my efforts failed."[55] Likewise, Jeff Lewis, the California real estate investor, admits to being preoccupied with perfection. If the bottles of water in his home refrigerator are not all lined up in order, with their labels facing out, he will throw a tantrum. However, Lewis believes his obsessive-compulsive personality disorder works to his advantage. In real estate sales, there are hundreds of tiny details that must be met or the sale could fall through. Lewis's attention to detail has helped make sure his sales are always successful. "OK, I have a mental affliction," he says. "But it's an asset. My perfectionism sets my product apart."[56]

Lewis is the rare sufferer of a personality disorder who has found a way to channel his quirky behavior toward a useful goal. For most people, though, personality disorders typically result in strained or broken relationships, little success in school, roadblocks to career advancement, substance abuse, and other societal ills. In many cases, personality disorders can also lead to physical abuse and even death for those who suffer from the disorders as well as for those who are unfortunate enough to cross their paths.

CHAPTER FOUR

Can Personality Disorders Be Controlled?

What sets people who suffer from personality disorders apart from other mental health patients is the difficulties they pose to the people who try to help them. For starters, most people who suffer from personality disorders do not believe they have a problem. People with paranoid personality disorders do not believe or trust what others say about them, so they do not take to heart a friend's suggestion to seek help. Other people with personality disorders are also in denial. "People rarely come in with a self-diagnosed personality disorder," says Adelphi University psychologist Lawrence Josephs. "Friends and family push them into it."[57]

When the personality disorder sufferers finally do seek professional help, they tend to be reluctant patients. They spar with their psychotherapists, refusing to believe the diagnoses. Often, they do not believe their therapists understand their problems. As psychotherapist Joel Paris explains, "When you're the therapist, you start feeling that you must be a terrible therapist to have somebody hate you or telling you such things as 'I'm going to kill myself, and it's your fault, Doctor.'"[58]

Moreover, antidepressant drugs are believed to offer mixed results to people with personality disorders. Some personality

Doctors find people with personality disorders to be in denial about their condition, making them highly resistant to psychotherapy.

disorder patients are able to control their quirky behavior with the help of drugs. In other patients, however, drugs have little value. Still, by working with their doctors and following a program that includes many different therapies, some people can learn how to control their tendencies to act abnormally in what are otherwise normal social situations. In most cases, the first step they take is to learn how to talk about their problems.

Talk Therapy

Talk therapy, in which a psychotherapist encourages the patient to discuss what troubles him or her, has been employed by therapists since Sigmund Freud pioneered the technique more than a century ago. During talk therapy, the psychiatrist or psychologist attempts to form a bond that will enhance the comfort level of the patient, helping him or her recall troubling events in the past. The therapist and patient may explore the patient's dreams, daydreams, thoughts, desires, moods, and aspirations in order to get to the root of the patient's problems. It may take years of psychotherapy and self-exploration before the patient finally opens up and learns the true source of his or her troubles.

Mental health professionals find that talk therapy can be a help to people with personality disorders, but the sessions are often difficult and combative and are regarded by therapists as just one component of a patient's treatment program. For example, narcissists typically think they have all the answers. They may tell the doctor that they feel fine and they have agreed to come in just to get husbands or wives to stop nagging them. They are pompous and may explode in angry tirades when confronted with the truth. "They come in under duress," says Josephs. "But they don't commit. What they really want is to have everything on their own terms."[59]

Borderlines, on the other hand are very willing to tell their stories: In fact, they are so willing to pour out their troubles that therapists find they can often diagnose borderline personality disorder within a few minutes of speaking with the patients. "I can sometimes do it in ten minutes," says Paris. "There is a feel about these people. . . . When most people see a psychiatrist, they open up slowly. Borderlines will give you deep stuff in minutes."[60]

Narcissists and Therapy

Narcissists are among the most difficult patients to convince to seek help. Indeed, the very nature of their ailment makes narcissists believe there is nothing wrong with them—they think they are smarter than everyone else, so why should they believe what others tell them?

When they are diagnosed with a narcissistic personality, their treatment is often long and difficult. Narcissistic patients fight against the diagnosis and are uncooperative during talk therapy. They may know something is wrong, but their general nature is to be defensive and deceptive. Thus, they have a great deal of trouble accepting advice and guidance from their therapists.

In many cases, spouses and other family members push narcissists into therapy. Narcissists do initiate treatment on their own, but not because they have recognized the symptoms of narcissism in themselves. Usually, after their careers or personal relationships take a downward slide—for reasons they blame on others—patients will become depressed and seek the help of mental health professionals. "That's when they come to see someone like me," says Robert Nebrosky, a San Diego, California, psychotherapist who specializes in treating narcissists. "At some point, they look around and realize that at home, and at work, everyone hates them."

Quoted in Benedict Carey, "Narcissist Anguish: I Loathe Myself for Loving Me," *Bergen County (NJ) Record*, October 20, 2002, p. F-1.

Antisocials are known to resist psychotherapy. According to Len Sperry, a professor of psychiatry at the Medical College of Wisconsin, antisocials are often very open to talking about themselves and what troubles them, but they also tend to lie and become manipulative. It is common for antisocials to respond in anger when their psychotherapists challenge their stories. "It is very difficult to have them focus on their impulsivity, irresponsibility or the negative consequences of their actions,"[61] says Sperry.

Depending on their specific personality disorder, patients in talk therapy may exhibit behaviors such as being too talkative, too combative, or too withdrawn to open up about their problems.

Avoidants offer a very different type of resistance to talk therapy. By their nature, avoidants are shy and uncomfortable around others. Convincing avoidants to open up about themselves can turn into a long and frustrating labor for the doctor. Obsessive-compulsives, on the other hand, sometimes talk too much, dwelling on insignificant issues in their lives. "Their preoccupation with and focus on details and need for control lead to a seemingly endless struggle about words, issues, and who is in charge without being able to develop an atmosphere of understanding and cooperation,"[62] says Sperry.

Paranoids feel threatened and do not trust others; they are also very secretive and prone to fits of anger—all of which can pose some enormous challenges for the therapists who are attempting to win the trust of their patients. "Their treatment is not easy but requires empathy, patience, and a great deal of sensitivity to their vulnerabilities,"[63] says Sperry.

Different Challenges

Despite the challenges psychotherapists face when dealing with different personality disorders, in all cases the therapists have the same goals: to convince their patients to talk about themselves and their troubles and to try to find the root causes of their personality disorders. To accomplish this, the psychotherapists may try to take their patients back in time. Since most personality disorders are believed to have their roots in childhood, patients are encouraged to talk about the traumatic events of their youths that may have triggered their personality disorders. It can be a difficult phase of the therapy because many patients have had troubled childhoods that have included physical, sexual, or psychological abuse.

Sometimes, the spark that caused the personality disorder can be a distant memory of what, to the patient, seemed like a minor and obscure incident in his or her childhood. Psychologists Francine Shapiro and Philip Manfield have written about a case involving a patient they call Mr. A, a man in his forties who was diagnosed as avoidant and schizoid. Mr. A's therapist led him through several talk therapy sessions, learning that Mr. A's parents were probably both narcissistic and demanding. In addition, the patient maintained a close relationship with a grandmother, who was also narcissistic. In interviewing Mr. A, the therapist learned that Mr. A's parents and grandmother often berated and criticized him when he failed to live up to their expectations. After many sessions, the therapist helped the patient explore an incident in his childhood in which the grandmother had given money for ice cream to Mr. A's cousins, but not to Mr. A.

"Mr. A internalized these experiences as meaning there was something wrong with him or that he was bad, although he couldn't figure out why he would deserve this treatment," write Shapiro and Manfield. "The image he thought of was of his

Personality disorders may be triggered by dim memories of traumatic experiences suffered in childhood.

cousins standing around the ice cream truck excitedly buying their ice cream pops and him standing by himself watching. His negative cognition was, 'I'm not lovable.'"[64] That single incident was probably not the sole cause for Mr. A developing traits of the avoidant and the schizoid, but it gave the therapist a clear idea of how Mr. A perceived himself and the type of home environment in which he lived. Finding the root causes of Mr. A's troubles helped the therapist bring Mr. A out of his shell. After a period of fifteen months, Mr. A felt his self-esteem had improved, and he was more comfortable in relationships and social situations he previously found uncomfortable as an avoidant and schizoid.

As therapists diagnose their patients and begin talk therapy, they must decide how best to approach their treatments. For example, doctors have found it is better to be less confrontational with schizoid and schizotypal clients, who are suspicious of others and tolerate less emotional probing. On the other hand, they may go right at borderline clients, who need to be confronted and made to realize their behavior is dangerous.

Convincing borderlines that their behavior is self-destructive is often difficult to accomplish. According to Paris:

> Usually, borderline patients are very demanding of therapy. The irony is, and this has been shown in research, that if you offer borderlines psychotherapy, about two-thirds of them will drop out within a few months—another measure of their impulsivity and emotional instability. In other words, they get frustrated with the therapist. They might say to the therapist, "You're not helping me. You don't care," then storm out.[65]

Group Therapy

Talk therapy is not necessarily limited to one-on-one sessions between patients and therapists. Many therapists find progress can be made during group therapy sessions, in which many patients who share similar symptoms discuss their common problems among themselves. The sessions are supervised by psychotherapists, who believe group therapy can help their

How Do Borderlines Endure the Pain?

Borderlines often react to stress by cutting themselves with razor blades or other sharp objects. Mental health experts have often been puzzled by the behavior. They have wondered why borderline patients would continue to endure the pain of self-mutilation.

Recent studies suggest that the body includes natural chemicals that dull the pain during certain types of injuries. Doctors liken the chemicals to opiates, the chemicals found in most painkillers as well as in many illegal narcotics. Long-distance runners and other athletes often find themselves exhilarated by these natural opiates. When many athletes reach what they believe are the limits of their physical endurance, they suddenly find a new reservoir of strength in their bodies that enables them to continue. Doctors have suggested that self-mutilators have also experienced similar natural "highs," and that is why the pain of cutting themselves does not seem to be a deterrent.

"When I would cut myself deliberately, I didn't even feel it," Emily, a sixteen-year-old borderline patient at a psychiatric hospital in Cambridge, Massachusetts, tells *Time*. "But if I got a paper cut I didn't want, that would hurt." Adds New York psychologist Jennifer Hartstein, "The longer kids cut, the more they need it."

Quoted in Jeffrey Kluger, "The Cruelest Cut," *Time*, May 16, 2005, p. 48.

patients examine their own lives if they hear other patients talk about similar issues.

Of course, group therapy offers its own set of challenges to the psychotherapist. It can take little to spark an angry or violent outburst by an antisocial; therefore, if a therapist gathers eight or ten antisocials in the same room at the same time, care must be taken to keep tempers in check. Sperry advocates picking the members of the group very carefully, and he suggests that perhaps two therapists should keep an eye on things.

Similarly, therapists have found they have to carefully monitor group sessions involving histrionics because histrionics often put each other under stress. Some psychotherapists hold the opinion that histrionics are so disruptive that group therapy simply does not work for them, but Sperry says that group sessions can be beneficial for these patients by helping self-centered histrionics understand the needs of others.

Unlike the participants in this group therapy session, patients suffering from personality disorders have volatile personalities, presenting therapists with special challenges when treating them in groups.

Group therapy also can be effective in treating avoidants—providing that the therapists can convince the avoidants to attend the group sessions. After all, avoidants do not like to participate in social situations or talk about themselves in front of others. Perhaps a psychotherapist can slowly draw an avoidant out of his or her shell after months of individual therapy in which the therapist and patient have had an opportunity to bond: Convincing the avoidant to open up in front of a group of strangers is a much more formidable task. Still, Sperry believes that avoidants can benefit from group therapy. The social situation of group therapy, he says, can help them make friends and learn social skills that they can use at work, in school, or in other settings.

Obsessive-compulsive patients may also do well in group sessions. Although psychotherapists have found that, in many cases, one or more of the participants tend to dominate the others during group sessions, Sperry believes the therapy can help obsessive-compulsives. Sperry has found that obsessive-compulsives are often open to accepting feedback from others—in fact, one of the traits of obsessive-compulsive personality order is listening to too many opinions, even if the obsessive-compulsive ultimately takes no one's advice. Sperry suggests group therapy can be a way in which an obsessive-compulsive begins to take other people's advice to heart. "Because a major deficit of the obsessive-compulsive personality is the inability to share tenderly and spontaneously with others, group treatment has particular advantages with such patients,"[66] he says.

However, there are some personality disorder patients who generally do not respond well to group therapy. For example, there have been few attempts made by therapists to establish group sessions for schizotypals. Since they often live in fantasy worlds, many therapists do not see the benefit of schizotypals sharing their fantasies with one another. Sperry, however, suggests that group therapy can be beneficial if the patients can be convinced to recognize each other's fantasies for what they are: fantasies. "Obviously," he says, "appropriate selection of which schizotypal patients will benefit from being in a group is an important task."[67]

Antidepressants and Antipsychotics

Whether they participate in individual talk therapy sessions with their doctors or in group sessions, many personality disorder patients do need something extra to help them open up and stay relaxed and focused. For many years, psychiatrists have prescribed antidepressant medications for their personality disorder patients. Results vary, usually depending on the disorder.

Antidepressant drugs block or enhance the neurotransmitters, the chemicals manufactured by the brain that control mood. The neurotransmitter serotonin, for example, regulates a person's mood as well as other physical effects and mental desires, such as sex drive, sleep, appetite, attention, and pain. A person whose brain manufactures too little serotonin may often feel depressed or anxious. To treat a depressed person, a psychiatrist will often prescribe an antidepressant drug, such as Prozac, to enhance the flow of serotonin in the brain.

Psychiatrists may prescribe antidepressant drugs to patients with personality disorders, but drugs alone do not seem to provide long-term control over their emotions. Unlike depression and anxiety, there seem to be other factors, including genetics, home environment, and childhood memories, that drive personality disorders and not just imbalances in the neurotransmitters that control mood.

Antidepressant drugs seem to work best for patients who suffer from avoidant personality disorder. The symptoms of avoidant personality disorder are very similar to the symptoms of social phobia, in which people harbor irrational fears of being in social situations and interacting with others. Antidepressant drugs have been found to be effective in reducing stress in social phobia patients, and psychiatrists have found them to have similar value for avoidant personality disorder patients. "The results [have] demonstrated the disappearance of the physical manifestations of social anxiety, as well as an increased comfort and initiative in work and social settings,"[68] says Sperry. Since schizoids often exhibit symptoms similar to those suffered by avoidants, psychiatrists have found positive

Avoidants and people with social phobias may be helped by taking antidepressant drugs; however, such medications are ineffective in treating other personality disorders.

results when they prescribe antidepressants to their schizoid patients.

Since schizotypals often exhibit symptoms similar to schizophrenia, psychiatrists have prescribed antipsychotic drugs to their schizotypal patients. Antipsychotic drugs, which revolutionized the treatment of schizophrenia, block the brain's release of another neurotransmitter, dopamine, which also regulates mood, particularly happiness. Since schizotypal behavior is not regarded as severe as that occuring in schizophrenia, doctors typically prescribe low doses of antipsychotic drugs to their schizotypal patients.

For other personality disorder patients, though, drugs may not provide much relief. According to Sperry, there are no drugs that have been recommended to treat dependent or obsessive-compulsive personality disorders. Meanwhile, psychiatrists have tried a wide variety of antidepressant drugs on borderline patients and have found few effective medications. At first, borderline patients seem to respond well to drug therapy, but eventually the drugs become less effective, probably because the disorder has its roots in childhood trauma and similar factors rather than a neurotransmitter imbalance. As Paris explains:

> Borderlines don't respond to drugs very well, even though most of them are on medication. At this point in time, pharmacological treatment doesn't last long and is not very impressive. If I give Prozac to somebody with classic depression, it's almost like magic. The patient often feels like a new person in a few weeks. But if I give borderline patients Prozac, they might feel a little better, yet in a few weeks we'll be back to square one. Although drugs are given to many of these patients, we haven't discovered or haven't invented the right one yet.[69]

No Wonder Drugs

According to Sperry, since drugs have limited value for personality disorders, doctors simply have to find the drug therapy that seems to work best for their patients. "Medication treatment . . . is largely trial and error," says Sperry. "That is because, generally speaking, there are not specific drug treatments for specific personality disorders."[70]

While there are no wonder drugs that can cure or control personality disorders, psychiatrists have found that some drugs can be effective in controlling the type of behavior that patients often exhibit. Psychiatrists can prescribe drugs to make patients less aggressive, angry, and moody. In paranoids, for example, antidepressant drugs have been found to help control their feelings of suspiciousness and irritability. In narcissists, antidepressants have helped some patients feel more empathetic toward others. But paranoids and narcissists suffer from other unpleasant behavioral traits, so the antidepressant drugs may not resolve all their symptoms.

The drug lithium has been used to treat the wild mood swings and hyperactive behavior exhibited by many mental patients.

Psychiatrists have prescribed it for antisocials with mixed results. It seems to calm them down, but antisocials often do not do a very good job of taking their pills when they are supposed to.

Sandy Naiman, a histrionic patient from Toronto, Canada, said she took large doses of lithium for many years and found the drug had little effect on her personality—she still found herself living through mood swings. "Lithium never really worked for me," she says. "If I was down, I was never clinically depressed, never suicidal, just normally sad, blue, unhappy, as all of us are from time to time, though my tendency to dramatize always made things seem worse than they were."[71]

Even in cases where lithium or similar drugs do successfully deaden the impulses and other bizarre behaviors of personality disorder patients, the drugs are not treating the illness, just making the symptoms less severe. Still, if drugs provide even a small measure of help, the patients may be convinced that their treatments are working, and they may be more willing to comply with other components of their therapies.

Important First Step

Talk therapy, group therapy, and antidepressant drugs can all help control the symptoms of personality disorders. Mental health experts have concluded, though, that there is no single blanket cure that can treat all personality disorder patients. Rather, they believe strongly that the needs of each patient must be assessed and an individual treatment program structured to his or her needs.

In addition, what often complicates treatment is that some patients may suffer from more than one personality disorder. In such cases, the therapists truly have to formulate individual strategies that may take a long time to refine, as the therapists and patients both go through periods of trial and error. Sperry says, "The more treatment can be tailored to a specific client, the more likely it is to be effective, and tailoring involves much more than matching a treatment method to a specific personality disorder."[72] Certainly, a patient who suffers from more than one personality disorder would present something of a

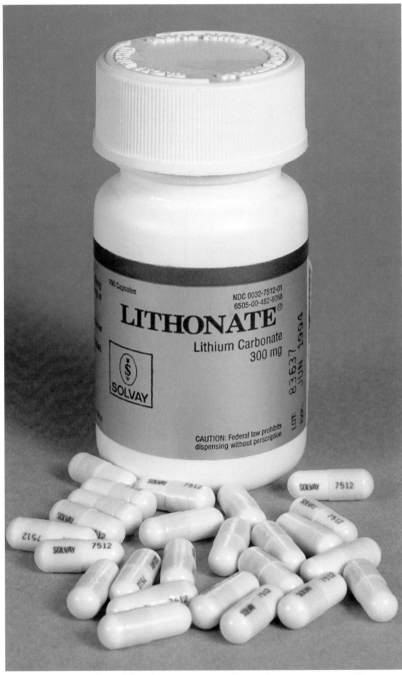

Lithium-based drugs like this one may relieve the symptoms of some mental patients, but they do not treat the illness itself.

challenge to a doctor who may seek to tackle the symptoms through drug therapy: A drug that works on a patient's schizotypal tendencies may have little effect on the same patient's borderline behavior.

There is no question that the treatment of personality disorder patients can be long, frustrating, and challenging to psychotherapists. For families and friends, getting the personality disorder patients to admit the truth about their afflictions to themselves, and begin treatment, remains the most important first step.

CHAPTER FIVE

New Therapies, Future Hopes

Since drug therapy and psychotherapy often produce limited results for personality disorder patients, mental health experts have looked to a new treatment technique that may hold a lot of promise for people with personality disorders, particularly borderline patients. Known as dialectical behavior therapy (DBT), the treatment seeks to teach patients how to cope with what troubles them. Borderlines, for example, often react to stress by cutting themselves or taking even more drastic steps, such as attempting suicide. In DBT, the patient learns to find other ways to react to stress.

Indeed, many personality disorder patients simply need an outlet for their stresses and frustrations. Under DBT, they may be encouraged to take up painting, write down their feelings, or even bake a cake. In other words, they are encouraged to engage in creative outlets that do not involve mutilation or other self-destructive activities. There is, of course, more to DBT than just learning how to paint or bake: To overcome what troubles them, people in DBT programs typically spend hours in individual and group sessions with psychotherapists, probing the roots of their problems and learning to recognize the warning signs that might send them spiraling back into self-destructive behavior. Says University of Washington psychologist

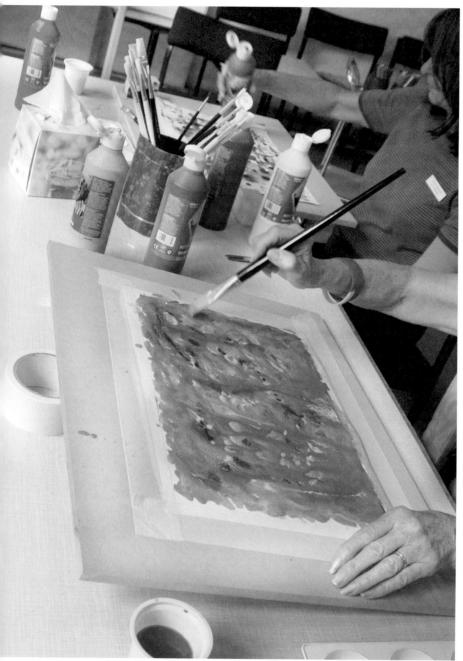

Dialectical behavior therapy (DBT) includes teaching coping skills to personality disorder patients and may include such activities as painting to relieve their stress.

Marsha Linehan, a pioneer in DBT therapy, "The first thing we teach is to get control of their behavior. After that, we work on feeling better."[73]

Meanwhile, other researchers are taking a different approach to attacking personality disorders. They are studying the anatomy of the brain, searching for clues that might suggest that personality disorders have biological causes. If it can be established that a personality disorder is caused by a brain defect, there is also hope that drug treatments or other therapies can be tailored specifically to the biological causes of the disorders.

Truth Through Discussion

Dialectical behavior therapy—*dialectical* means "seeking truth through discussion"—is similar to cognitive behavior therapy, which has been employed by therapists for more than fifty years, typically to treat people who suffer from phobias and other irrational fears. A person who fears heights, for example, would be encouraged in his or her first session to take an elevator ride to the second floor. After getting comfortable on the second floor, the patient would be encouraged in the next session to ride up to the third or fourth floors. Eventually, after several sessions, the patient should be able to handle an elevator ride to the top of a skyscraper.

Cognitive behavior therapy helps the patients confront what troubles them while gradually finding ways to overcome those issues. In other words, cognitive behavior therapy is all about setting goals and finding ways to reach them. A person too depressed to get out of bed in the morning may start cognitive behavior therapy by moving the alarm clock so that he or she would have to get out of bed to turn it off. That way, the depressed person takes the first few steps toward overcoming the feeling of anxiety that prevents him or her from getting out of bed. On the second day, the patient may be encouraged to place the clock all the way across the room, perhaps next to the clothes closet, so that he or she has to take several steps to turn it off. On the third day, the patient may be encouraged to get dressed.

Health Insurance and Personality Disorders

Psychotherapy can be expensive, often costing clients several hundred dollars an hour. In the United States, most health care is paid by insurance companies that cover workers and their families under the benefits plans offered to workers by their employers. Health insurance plans typically cover psychiatric illnesses, but because treatment of personality disorders has such a low level of success, many insurance companies have balked at paying for patients' therapies. As a result, many personality disorder patients go untreated because they cannot afford to pay the doctors out of their own pockets. "For the most part, insurers think personality disorders are a lost cause—something they don't want to cover," says Cleveland, Ohio, psychologist James Pretzer.

Psychiatrists and psychologists hope to change that thinking. When they accept new patients, many place calls to the insurance companies themselves and argue on behalf of the new clients, suggesting that their patients can go on to develop much more serious mental illnesses if their personality disorders go untreated. Ironically, those disorders, such as depression and schizophrenia, would be fully covered by the benefits plans, but they may be very expensive to treat—particularly if the patient is required to be institutionalized.

Quoted in Karen Kersting, "Axis II Gets Short Shrift," *Monitor on Psychology*, March 2004, p. 50.

In DBT, the principle is much the same. Working together, the therapist and personality disorder patient develop a set of goals for the patient to achieve. As part of working toward those goals, the therapist will help the patient learn better social skills. Also, patients are taught coping and problem-solving skills. Typically, patients work with their therapists for a year or more, participating in individual sessions as well as group sessions. During

DBT, particularly in the group sessions, the participants are taught to be nonjudgmental—no one should be belittled or criticized for cutting themselves or responding in other impulsive or self-destructive ways to stressful situations. Instead, the patients realize that their problems are very real, but they have chosen the wrong ways to cope with them. Harold Koenigsberg, an associate professor of psychiatry at Mount Sinai School of Medicine in New York, says, "The brain of the borderline person is fine-tuned to overreact to negative emotion."[74]

Linehan has developed DBT to address the unique problems of the borderline patient. At the beginning of DBT, the patient sets a goal—to not resort to self-destructive behavior either through cutting, suicide attempts, or engaging in other harmful acts such as substance abuse. The patient is made to understand that cutting has been a coping skill, and that he or she must find another way to cope.

Looking for Red Flags

Setting goals and learning coping skills are important steps in DBT, but learning how to recognize the type of stressful situations that cause self-destructive behavior is perhaps the most important skill the patient will acquire. After beginning DBT, the patient and therapist start looking for the red flags that signal trouble is ahead—the sparks that ignite the stress a borderline patient feels. When one of those red flags is raised, the patient is encouraged to call the therapist to talk over the proper reaction to the situation.

For example, if a borderline teenage girl has an argument with her boyfriend, her initial reaction may be to cut herself as a way of coping with her emotional stress. The red flag is the argument: Before cutting herself, the patient is instructed to call the therapist, who suggests other ways to cope with the trauma caused by the argument. Perhaps the girl may be encouraged to call her boyfriend back to see if they can resolve their differences. Or the borderline may be encouraged to call and talk things over with a girlfriend or close family member. Perhaps the therapist will simply suggest the borderline take a hot bath or walk around the block. Linehan says, "You have to get these people not to go to the hospital when they're feeling suicidal and at the same time have them feel they're not being left on the floor, that they have some skills to manage."[75]

The patients are asked to do homework, usually to keep diaries in which they record their reactions to stressful situations. When the girl argued with her boyfriend, did she respond by cutting herself? Or did she just relax in a hot bath as a way of relieving her stress? In their diaries, the patients are urged to record the events that led up to the stressful incidents as a way of identifying the red flags that could prompt them in the future to cut themselves.

When the patients slip into thoughts of harming themselves, they are instructed to call their therapists for support. Later,

A therapist (right) counsels a young woman. In DBT therapy, therapists help patients with personality disorders learn to recognize the red flags that trigger stress.

Skeptical Views of Dialectical Behavior Therapy

Proponents of dialectical behavior therapy (DBT) believe it is effective in helping borderline patients control their impulsive behaviors. Under DBT, patients are taught positive coping strategies for dealing with the stresses in their lives. Typically, DBT lasts about a year.

The therapy was conceived by psychologists at the University of Washington, who claim that the suicide rate for borderline patients in DBT is half the rate for all borderline patients in the United States. (According to the New York–based Borderline Personality Disorder Research Foundation, between 3 and 9.5 percent of all borderline patients take their lives each year.) Based on those results, some states have mandated DBT training for mental health professionals who treat borderline patients.

There are skeptics of DBT, though. Drew Westen, a professor of psychiatry at Emory University in Atlanta, Georgia, suggests that more study is needed. "It concerns me that so many states are mandating this treatment when we only have year-long studies, and we don't know if it really eliminates the problem long term," he says. "My guess would be that the problems (borderlines) have in the experience of the self, the emptiness and abandonment they feel, probably aren't going to change much in one year." Critics also suggest that DBT may seem to work because the therapists give clients more attention than the patients would otherwise receive in different types of psychotherapy, and DBT therapists are very motivated because of their high confidence in what they are doing.

Quoted in Benedict Carey, "With Toughness and Caring, a Novel Therapy Helps Tortured Souls," *New York Times*, July 13, 2004, p. F-1.

they must recount for the therapist the exact circumstances under which they went from feeling fine to feeling suicidal.

Not Really a Cure

DBT is not really a cure; rather, when a borderline patient enters DBT, he or she has accepted the diagnosis and is looking for a way to manage the symptoms. DBT patients may also undergo talk therapy and group therapy, but usually those stages in their therapies occur after they have learned coping skills in DBT. Essentially, the goal of DBT is to help the borderline patient manage his or her impulsive behavior before the therapist begins the process of getting to the root of the patient's problems. Indeed, practitioners of DBT realize, especially with borderlines, that these patients are often self-destructive and suicidal, so helping them manage their troubles may be more important, in the short term, than finding out what may be truly troubling them.

Some therapists believe DBT can help more than just borderline patients. Len Sperry of the Medical College of Wisconsin believes avoidants can be convinced to work toward goals as they learn to interact with others and become more comfortable in social situations. Dependents can also learn to work toward goals as they become more independent. Histrionics often have difficulty in maintaining independent lives as well, and Sperry believes setting goals can help them, too. "Challenging their most basic assumption such as 'I am inadequate and have to rely on others to survive,' is aided by cognitive-behavior methods such as assertion and problem-solving [that] help them feel more competent,"[76] he says. Obsessive-compulsives also respond well to DBT therapy; their coping skills may involve learning how to be more sensitive to others.

The goal for a schizotypal may be learning to realize his or her bizarre thoughts have no basis in reality. "As they learn to disregard inappropriate thoughts, they are able to consider the consequences that responding emotionally or behaviorally to such thoughts would have, and they can respond more rationally,"[77] says Sperry.

Psychologist Judith Beck of Bala Cynwyd, Pennsylvania, employed the principles of DBT in her treatment of a narcissis-

A counselor meets with a patient. DBT therapists work with borderline patients who have accepted their diagnosis and are seeking ways to cope with their disorder.

tic patient. The patient, a retired corporate executive, had always been treated with respect and deference by his employees. After retiring, the man found it difficult to adjust to life without underlings seeing to his every wish. If the man thought he was not given proper respect at the dry cleaner's, the grocery store, or the library checkout counter, he would become defensive and explode in a tirade.

Working together, Beck and the patient developed a set of coping skills for such situations. Rather than chewing them out, Beck counseled her patient to engage people in conversation—to ask them about their jobs, their likes and dislikes, their hobbies, and their home lives. After interacting with others, Beck says, the patient found them to be generally warm people who meant him no disrespect. "He was flabbergasted at the response," she says. "No one attacked him; people reacted very positively. This went a long way in changing his idea that he had to always be on guard."[78]

Biological Reasons

Convincing personality disorder patients to find positive ways to cope with their impulsive and self-destructive behaviors can go a long way toward helping them live normal lives. While psychotherapists find new coping strategies for patients, other mental health professionals are exploring new avenues that could help patients control their personality disorders. For the most part, these scientists are looking at the possible biological causes of personality disorders, concentrating on defects in the brain or other parts of their bodies that may be causing patients to behave abnormally.

If a biological reason for a personality disorder can be established, research scientists and doctors can work together to develop cures, perhaps in the form of new medications. Such methods to control or cure personality disorders may be years in the future; nevertheless, by gaining a better understanding of the biological reasons for personality disorders, scientists hope to take important steps toward finding cures.

Anybody who has been in a stressful situation—a confrontation with a bully, opening night of a school play, a first date with a potential new girlfriend or boyfriend—usually knows it because he or she can feel a racing heartbeat. In most people, antisocial behavior—such as vandalism, cheating on a test, or shoplifting—should cause a racing heartbeat as well. Studies have shown that antisocial men have slow heartbeats, indicating that they have muted responses to stress. In other words, they lack a racing heart that tells them what they are doing may be wrong.

Some scientists suggest that the brains of antisocial patients may suffer from a deficiency of norepinephrine, a neurotransmitter produced by the brain that helps the body react to stress. According to neurobiologist Debra Niehoff:

The reason antisocial aggressors "just don't get it"— regardless of social disapproval, personal failure, even incarceration—may be related to the [lack of norepineph-rine], an insensitivity suggested by their damped down heart rates and confirmed by their half-hearted responses to stress. Without the emotional arousal that normally locks environmental cues to outcomes, the antisocial individual never learns to anticipate the consequences of his aggression or that his actions have an impact on the welfare of others. Instead, his complacent nervous system betrays him over and over again to the same mistakes, while his inability to comprehend the feelings of others progressively erodes social relationships.[79]

If the antisocial patient suffers from a lack of norepineph-rine, why not just find a drug that induces the brain to release more norephineprhine? According to Niehoff, boosting the brain's output of norepinephrine may not achieve the desired result. She suggests that tweaking the flow of norepinephrine in the brain of an antisocial may affect how other neurotransmitters regulate the patient's moods and emotions. "Pushing the . . . norepinephrine system to its limits elevates daily interaction with the world from a struggle for existence to a pitched battle for survival, a perpetual conflict with an environment that seems not only unsafe but unpleasant," says Niehoff. "When every encounter represents a threat and every experience is disagreeable, can it be any wonder that hostility is the end result?"[80]

With so much mystery surrounding how neurotransmitters affect antisocials and other personality disorder patients, it may take years of more study before a drug can be developed that makes antisocials less likely to engage in impulsive behavior. Still, the recent studies have given scientists a lot more understanding about antisocials and why they often act as they do—an important first step in finding an effective treatment for them.

Physical Evidence

As research continues on the role of neurotransmitters in the behavior of personality disorder patients, some scientists are

A person suffering from an antisocial disorder feels continually threatened and is likely to lash out violently.

concentrating more on the brain's actual components. Recent personality disorder studies have looked at the parts of the brain known as the amygdalae and prefrontal cortex.

The amygdalae are two tiny, almond-shaped balls of tissue found near the center of the brain near the ears. The amygdalae control human emotions. When a situation prompts an emotional response in a person, the amygdalae activate a number of physical reactions in the body, such as a faster heartbeat, a rise in blood pressure, perspiration through the sweat glands, and perhaps a churning feeling in the stomach.

The amygdalae kick-start the fight-or-flight response: the reaction all people have to emotional situations. During a tense and fearful encounter with another person, the fight-or-flight response will influence a person's decision to stay and make a fight of it (either verbally or physically) or to walk away.

In a 2007 study reported in the *American Journal of Psychiatry*, the amygdalae in personality disorder patients were shown to be overreacting as the patients studied the neutral expressions on the faces of volunteers, suggesting that their negative reactions are prompted by misinterpreted communications. Researchers believe that overactive amygdalae will make the patient more prone to acting on impulse. Antisocials, for example, may react to the fight-or-flight response by acting on their impulse to fight rather than taking the more sensible approach of walking away from volatile situations. Overactive amygdalae in borderline patients may prompt them to react to the fight-or-flight response by cutting themselves. The histrionic may throw a tantrum. The avoidant usually responds to a fight-or-flight situation by running away.

Some mental health experts believe studies of the amygdalae confirm that DBT and other cognitive behavior therapies can be effective in treating personality disorders. Since DBT seeks to replace impulsive behavior with better coping skills, therapists believe patients can rely on the skills they learn in DBT to help them gain control of their overactive amygdalae. As the *American Journal of Psychiatry* explains, "Results from this study suggest that the specific behavioral and brain mechanisms implicated in decreased impulse control in borderline personality disorder could be addressed by known treatments."[81]

Another section of the brain that has been studied for its effect on personality disorders is the prefrontal cortex, which is found in the front of the brain just behind the eyes. The prefrontal cortex controls rational and analytical thought. "The prefrontal cortex is like the guardian angel of behavior," says Adrian Raine, a professor of psychology at the University of Pennsylvania in Philadelphia. "It's the part of the brain that says, 'Hey, hold on a minute.'"[82]

In 2007 Raine headed a study that photographed the prefrontal cortexes of more than fourteen hundred people, including many convicted killers as well as others who have exhibited antisocial behavior. Results of the study found abnormalities in the prefrontal cortexes of the antisocials. Raine's study recommended no specific treatments for people with abnormal prefrontal cortexes, but the research could be important in helping therapists diagnose antisocial behavior. Now, as they assess what is wrong with their patients, they may be able to call on physical evidence as well as psychiatric evidence.

Making Progress

The recent studies of the amygdalae and prefrontal cortex show that science continues to reveal new truths about personality disorders. While it may be years before more effective drug treatments are available, therapies like DBT show that with hard work and dedication, many personality disorder patients can learn to control their impulsive behaviors. "Nobody totally changes," says Lawrence Josephs of Adelphi University. "But anyone can become more flexible. . . . Anyone can make progress."[83]

Still, there is no question that when it comes to personality disorders, all therapies are known to have limited results. A recent study conducted by John Gunderson of McLean Hospital and colleagues at Harvard, Yale, Columbia, and Brown universities found that only 40 percent of borderline, avoidant, obsessive-compulsive, and schizotypal patients who undergo a combination of talk therapy, drug therapy, and DBT show improvement after two years—meaning that 60 percent of patients show no improvement at all. While a 40 percent success rate may seem paltry to some, Gunderson is quick to add that therapies for personality disorder patients are still very much in their infancies. "That's big news," Gunderson says of the success rate for treating personality disorder patients. "Nobody would have thought we'd get better than 15 percent."[84]

Meanwhile, millions of other personality disorder patients are not seeking treatment. Indeed, many patients do not believe there is anything wrong with them. They can be found living, working, and going to school in American society, hiding from others, cutting themselves and engaging in other reckless and impulsive behaviors, exploding in fits of anger for the most trivial of reasons, convinced that only they know what truly troubles them.

Notes

Introduction: Personality Disorders: Widespread and Unpredictable

1. Quoted in Jeffrey Kluger and Sora Song, "Masters of Denial," *Time*, January 20, 2003, p. 84.
2. Mary Jo Fay, "Emotionally Hazardous Work Environments: What's the Health Care Cost?" *Medical News Today*, August 28, 2004. www.medicalnewstoday.com/articles/12599 .php.
3. Quoted in Laura Crimaldi, "Hot-Blooded Blueblood Jailed for Assault," *Boston Herald*, May 4, 2008. www.bostonherald .com/news/regional/general/view.bg?articleid=1091578&sr vc=home&position=1.
4. Quoted in Crimaldi, "Hot-Blooded Blueblood Jailed for Assault."

Chapter 1: What Are Personality Disorders?

5. Quoted in Patrick Perry, "Personality Disorders: Coping with the Borderline," *Saturday Evening Post*, July/August 1997, p. 44.
6. Quoted in Jeffrey J. Magnavita, ed., *Handbook of Personality Disorders: Theory and Practice*. Hoboken, NJ: John Wiley & Sons, 2004, p. 6.
7. Ronald Pies, "The Patient Who Saw the Future," *Boston Globe*, December 3, 2007, p. C-1.
8. Thomas Stuttaford, "No Symptoms of Ordinary Madness," *Times* (London), February 15, 2002, p. 17.
9. Quoted in Kluger and Song, "Masters of Denial," p. 84.
10. Quoted in Beth Sherman, "The Neighbor from Hell," *Newsday*, November 14, 1992, p. 17.
11. Randy K. Ward, "Assessment and Management of Personality Disorders," *American Family Physician*, October 15, 2004, p. 1505.

12. Quoted in Harriet Barovick, "Bad to the Bone," *Time*, December 19, 1999. www.time.com/time/magazine/article/0,91 71,36272,00.html.
13. Quoted in Jeffrey Kluger, "The Cruelest Cut," *Time*, May 16, 2005, p. 48.
14. Pamela Kulbarsh, "The Malignant Narcissist: Perverted Self-Love," *Officer*, April 20, 2008. www.officer.com/web/online/Police-Life/TheMalignant-Narcissist/17$41080.
15. Quoted in Nancy Kerchieval, "What, Not Who, Done It?" *Maryland Daily Record*, August 4, 2003.
16. Ward, "Assessment and Management of Personality Disorders," p. 1505.
17. Quoted in Joshua Kendall, "Famously Fussy," *Psychology Today*, March/April 2008, p. 43.
18. Quoted in Benedict Carey, "Insufferable Clinginess, or Health Dependence?" *New York Times*, March 6, 2007, p. F-1.
19. Quoted in Carey, "Insufferable Clinginess, or Health Dependence?" p. F-1.
20. Ward, "Assessment and Management of Personality Disorders," p. 1505.
21. Thomas Stuttaford, "I Want to Be Alone: The People Who Act Like Greta Garbo," *Times of London*, September 12, 2005, p. 14.
22. Magnavita, ed., *Handbook of Personality Disorders: Theory and Practice.* p. 7.
23. Quoted in Annie Murphy Paul, "Am I Normal?" *Psychology Today*, March/April 2005, p. 54.

Chapter 2: What Causes Personality Disorders?

24. R.C. Jebb, trans., *The Characters of Theophrastus*. www.eudaemonist.com/biblion/characters.
25. Debra Niehoff, *The Biology of Violence*. New York: Free Press, 1999, p. 153.
26. Gayleen L. McCoy and William E. Snell Jr., "Gender Role Tendencies and Personality Disorders," *Psi Chi Journal of Undergraduate Research*, Summer 2002, pp. 52–53.
27. Judy Gershon, "The Hidden Diagnosis," *USA Today* magazine, May 2007, p. 72.

28. Quoted in Sarah Ovaska, Jessica Fargen, and Chris Walker, "Sampson's Life a History of Violence," *Quincy (MA) Patriot Ledger*, August 1, 2001, p. 1.

29. Quoted in Dennis Tatz, "Jury Told Father Rejected Sampson," *Quincy (MA) Patriot Ledger*, December 4, 2003, p. 11.

30. Quoted in Shelley Murphy, "Doctor Says Killer Couldn't Stop Himself," *Boston Globe*, December 11, 2003, p. B-3.

31. Quoted in Kluger and Song, "Masters of Denial," p. 84.

32. Quoted in David Weber, "Defense Doc: Sampson Brain Abnormal Since Childhood," *Boston Herald*, December 10, 2003, p. 22.

33. Quoted in Weber, "Defense Doc," p. 22.

34. Quoted in Kluger and Song, "Masters of Denial," p. 84.

35. Magnavita, ed., *Handbook of Personality Disorders*, pp. 16–17.

36. Quoted in Joshua Kendall, "Famously Fussy," *Psychology Today*, March/April 2008, p. 43.

37. Alice Miller, *Prisoners of Childhood: The Drama of the Gifted and the Search for the True Self*. New York: Basic Books, 1987, pp. 5–6.

38. Quoted in Magnavita, ed., *Handbook of Personality Disorders*, p. 501.

39. Quoted in Charlotte Hoff, "Where Personality Goes Awry," *Monitor on Psychology*, March 2004, p. 42.

Chapter 3: Living with Personality Disorders

40. Quoted in George Rekers, *Susan Smith: Victim or Murderer?* Centennial, CO: Glenbridge, 1996, p. 55.

41. Terrell Owens and Stephen Singular, *Catch This: Going Deep with the NFL's Sharpest Weapon*. New York: Simon and Schuster, 2004, pp. 5–6.

42. Terrell Owens and Jason Rosenhaus, *T.O.* New York: Simon and Schuster, 2006, p. 137.

43. Tom Knott, "It's Not All About You, T.O.," *Washington Times*, November 16, 2005.

44. Dan Le Batard, "We All Share Fault for Being Owens' Enablers," *Miami Herald*, November 12, 2005.

45. Quoted in Michael Clarkson, "Addicted to Himself?" *Toronto Star*, January 8, 2004, p. E-3.

46. Quoted in Sally Jenkins, "Nobody Loves T.O. like T.O. Loves T.O.," *Washington Post*, November 10, 2005, p. E-1.

47. Murphy, "Am I Normal?" p. 54.

48. Quoted in Elizabeth Gleick, "A Life Beyond the Grave," *Time*, September 13, 1999, p. 76.

49. Quoted in Perry, "Personality Disorders," p. 44.

50. Quoted in Jordan Lite, "Borderlines We've Known, Loved— or Feared," *New York Daily News*, January 18, 2006, p. 2.

51. Quoted in Canadian Press, "Self-Inflicted Wounds on Teens a Suicide Warning for Parents," April 11, 2008. http://can adianpress.google.com/article/ALeqM5hDdi3Kn9R_ML8QF nHQhfiUCzsNUQ.

52. Quoted in Stanley A. Miller II, "Sucked Deep into Cyber-world Fantasy of EverQuest, Man Commits Suicide," *Mil-waukee Journal Sentinel*, April 8, 2002. www.accessmylib rary.com/coms2/summary_0286-8638075_ITM.

53. Quoted in Miller, "Sucked Deep into Cyberworld Fantasy of EverQuest, Man Commits Suicide."

54. Quoted in Associated Press, "Ex-GI Accused in Attack Had 'Anti-Social Personality Disorder,'" *USA Today*, July 6, 2006. www.usatoday.com/news/nation/2006-07-05-ex-soldier-charges _x.htm.

55. Quoted in Jennifer Magid, "Scene Stealers," *Psychology To-day*, October 2007, p. 45.

56. Quoted in Kendall, "Famously Fussy," p. 43.

Chapter 4: Can Personality Disorders Be Controlled?

57. Quoted in Kluger and Song, "Masters of Denial," p. 84.

58. Quoted in Perry, "Personality Disorders," p. 44.

59. Quoted in Kluger and Song, "Masters of Denial," p. 84.

60. Quoted in Perry, "Personality Disorders," p. 44.

61. Len Sperry, *Handbook of Diagnosis and Treatment of Person-ality Disorders*. New York: Brunner-Routledge, 2003, p. 48.

62. Sperry, *Handbook of Diagnosis and Treatment of Person-ality Disorders*, p. 184.

63. Sperry, *Handbook of Diagnosis and Treatment of Personality Disorders*, p. 210.

64. Quoted in Magnavita, ed., *Handbook of Personality Disorders*, p. 315.

65. Quoted in Perry, "Personality Disorders," p. 44.

66. Sperry, *Handbook of Diagnosis and Treatment of Personality Disorders*, p. 192.

67. Sperry, *Handbook of Diagnosis and Treatment of Personality Disorders*, p. 192.

68. Sperry, *Handbook of Diagnosis and Treatment of Personality Disorders*, p. 76.

69. Quoted in Perry, "Personality Disorders," p. 44.

70. Sperry, *Handbook of Diagnosis and Treatment of Personality Disorders*, p. 23.

71. Sandy Naiman, "Coming Out Crazy," *Chatelaine*, October 1999, p. 130.

72. Sperry, *Handbook of Diagnosis and Treatment of Personality Disorders*, p. 7.

Chapter 5: New Therapies, Future Hopes

73. Quoted in Kluger and Song, "Masters of Denial," p. 84.

74. Quoted in Jamie Talan, "The Ultimate Outsiders," *Newsday*, March 6, 2007, p. B-8.

75. Quoted in Benedict Carey, "So Far, Holding Up Under Scrutiny," *New York Times*, July 13, 2004, p. F-6.

76. Sperry, *Handbook of Diagnosis and Treatment of Personality Disorders*, p. 144.

77. Sperry, *Handbook of Diagnosis and Treatment of Personality Disorders*, p. 253.

78. Quoted in Benedict Carey, "Narcissist Anguish: I Loathe Myself for Loving Me," *Bergen County (NJ) Record*, October 20, 2002, p. F-1.

79. Niehoff, *The Biology of Violence*, p. 130.

80. Niehoff, *The Biology of Violence*, p. 133.

81. *American Journal of Psychiatry*, "Brain Mechanisms of Borderline Personality Disorder at the Intersection of Cognition, Emotion, and the Clinic," December 2007, p. 1778.

82. Quoted in Kathleen Fackelmann, "Sociopaths Could Be

Lacking a 'Guardian Angel of Behavior,'" *USA Today*, November 7, 2007, p. D-13.

83. Quoted in Kluger and Song, "Masters of Denial," p. 84.
84. Quoted in Kluger and Song, "Masters of Denial," p. 84.

Glossary

agoraphobia: Derived from the Greek word for "fear of the marketplace," agoraphobia is an irrational fear of leaving home. Many avoidants exhibit symptoms similar to those of agoraphobia.

antidepressant: This is a class of drugs that enhances the flow of neurotransmitters, the chemicals manufactured by the brain that regulate mood, emotion, and physical desire.

anxiety: A feeling of apprehension or tension that is common in most people who suffer from mental illnesses.

depression: A mental illness characterized by feelings of sadness, hopelessness, and inadequacy.

hallucinations: False images or sounds experienced by someone who suffers from schizotypal personality disorder, schizophrenia, or other mental illnesses. Many illegal drugs, including lysergic acid diethylamide (LSD), can also induce hallucinatory experiences.

neurobiologist: A research scientist who studies the brain, spinal cord, and nerves, which are the components of the body that make up the nervous system.

neurosis: A mental illness that manifests itself in feelings of anxiety and impulsive behavior. Many borderline personality disorder patients harbor symptoms similar to those of neurosis.

phobia: An irrational fear that often manifests itself in panic. A phobic person suffering from a fear of heights could lapse into a panic or similar response if he or she is forced to attend a meeting on an upper floor of a skyscraper.

psychiatrist: A physician who specializes in treating mental illnesses; unlike a psychologist, a psychiatrist is permitted to prescribe drugs.

psychologist: A professional who studies human behavior and provides therapy for patients with mental illnesses. Since psychologists have not attended medical schools, they are not permitted to prescribe drugs.

psychosis: A major mental illness in which the patient loses touch with reality and undergoes a dramatic change in his or her personality. Borderline personality disorder patients are in danger of slipping into psychosis.

psychotherapist: A professional, either a psychiatrist or a psychologist, who provides treatment for people suffering from mental illnesses. Most psychotherapists employ the techniques pioneered by Sigmund Freud more than a century ago.

schizophrenia: A mental illness similar to schizotypal personality disorder in which the patient suffers from an impaired vision of reality, often harboring bizarre delusions. Schizophrenia patients often hallucinate.

social phobia: An irrational fear of encountering people in social situations, such as work, school, parties, or other places where people gather. Social phobia is similar to avoidant personality disorder.

Organizations to Contact

American Psychiatric Association
1000 Wilson Blvd., Ste. 1825
Arlington, VA 22209-3901
phone: (888) 35-PSYCH
e-mail: apa@psych.org
Web site: www.psych.org

The organization serves as a professional association for more than thirty-eight thousand American psychiatrists. The association's *Diagnostic and Statistical Manual of Mental Disorders* is the primary resource employed by mental health professionals in diagnosing personality disorders in their patients. Visitors to the organization's Web site can find many articles written by association members about personality disorders.

American Psychological Association
750 First St. NE
Washington, DC 20002-4242
phone: (800) 374-2721
e-mail: public.affairs@apa.org
Web site: www.apa.org

The American Psychological Association represents more than 148,000 American psychologists. Students seeking information on personality disorders can find many articles on the subject written by leading American psychologists. In addition, the association has made its publication, *Monitor on Psychology*, available online. The magazine has featured many stories on personality disorders.

Borderline Personality Disorder Research Foundation
340 W. Twelfth St.
New York, NY 10014

phone: (212) 421-5244
fax: (212) 421-5243
e-mail: bpdrf.usa@verizon.net
Web site: www.borderlineresearch.org

Founded in 1999, the foundation organizes the activities of a number of agencies, hospitals, and similar groups that perform research into borderline personality disorder. Visitors to the organization's Web site can find information on the disorder as well as statistics on borderline patients. A number of publications about the personality disorder can be downloaded from the group's Internet site.

Borderline Personality Disorder Resource Center
New York–Presbyterian Hospital, Westchester Division
Banker Villa, Rm. 106
21 Bloomingdale Rd.
White Plains, NY 10605
phone: (888) 694-2273
e-mail: info@bpdresourcecenter.org
Web site: www.bpdresourcecenter.org

New York–Presbyterian Hospital's Borderline Personality Disorder Resource Center provides treatment to borderline patients. The organization's Web site offers many resources about the disorder, including a background on the illness, warning signs to look for in patients, and treatment options. Visitors to the organization's Web site can read the story of Pamela, a young borderline personality patient who took her own life.

Mental Health America
2000 N. Beauregard St., 6th Fl.
Alexandria, VA 22311
phone: (800) 969-6642
fax: (703) 684-5968
Web site: www.nmha.org

Mental Health America is an advocacy group for people with mental illnesses. The organization provides a referral service to help patients find therapists as well as contact information for suicide hotlines and other crisis intervention services that may benefit borderlines and other personality disorder patients who engage in self-destructive behavior.

National Alliance on Mental Illness (NAMI)
Colonial Place Three
2107 Wilson Blvd., Ste. 300
Arlington, VA 22201-3042
phone: (703) 524-7600
fax: (703) 524-9094
Web site: www.nami.org

The alliance is a national advocacy group for people with mental illnesses. NAMI's Web site includes many resources on borderline personality disorder as well as other personality disorders. By using the site's search engine, students can find an extensive library of news articles, press releases, congressional testimony, and other resources on personality disorders.

National Institute of Mental Health (NIMH)
6001 Executive Blvd.
Bethesda, MD 20892-9663
phone: (866) 615-6464
e-mail: nimhinfo@nih.gov
Web site: www.nimh.nih.gov

The NIMH is the federal government's chief funding agency for mental health research in America. Students can find many resources about personality disorders on the agency's Web site, including news updates on developments in treatment as well as summaries of research projects focusing on personality disorders.

For Further Reading

Books

Alex Chapman and Kim Gratz, *The Borderline Personality Disorder Survival Guide*. Oakland, CA: New Harbinger, 2007. The authors provide basic information about borderline personality disorder and review some of the treatments available to patients, including dialectical behavior therapy, psychotherapy, and antidepressant drug therapy.

Dusty Miller, *Women Who Hurt Themselves*. New York: Basic Books, 2004. The book includes an extensive discussion of borderline personality disorder and how it prompts people, particularly women and teenage girls, to self-mutilate.

Terrell Owens and Jason Rosenhaus, *T.O.* New York: Simon & Schuster, 2006. Terrell Owens, who published this autobiography soon after leaving the Philadelphia Eagles, gives his side of the story about what led to his very ugly and public dispute with the team. Owens also responds to what his critics have labeled narcissistic behavior and recounts episodes from his unhappy childhood.

Sally Bedell Smith, *Diana: In Search of Herself*. New York: Times, 1999. The author's biography of Princess Diana includes many episodes from Diana's life that suggest the late princess suffered from borderline personality disorder; the book recounts Diana's self-mutilation, her suspicious nature, and her emotional collapse.

Periodicals

Joshua Kendall, "Famously Fussy," *Psychology Today*, March/April 2008. Obsessive-compulsive personality disorder is examined in this magazine article, which argues that many obsessive-compulsives can lead productive lives if they learn how to manage their affliction and find ways to use it in their favor.

Jeffrey Kluger, "The Cruelest Cut," *Time*, May 16, 2005. The magazine article examines borderline personality disorder and how teenage girls often turn toward self-mutilation to cope with their stress; the benefits of dialectical behavior therapy are also examined in the story.

Jeffrey Kluger and Sora Song, "Masters of Denial," *Time*, January 20, 2003. The reporters provide an overview of personality disorders, discussing the genetic and environmental causes for the disorders as well as some of the therapies available for patients.

Annie Murphy Paul, "Am I Normal?" *Psychology Today*, March/April 2005. Paul, the author of the book *The Cult of Personality*, provides an overview of personality disorders and examines the case of a prosperous attorney whose career and personal life is disintegrating because of his antisocial tendencies.

Patrick Perry, "Personality Disorders: Coping with the Borderline," *Saturday Evening Post*, July/August 1997. The magazine article provides an extensive report on borderline personality disorder and the work of John Gunderson of McLean Hospital in Massachusetts in identifying the disorder in patients and developing therapies to treat them.

Jamie Talan, "The Ultimate Outsiders, People with Borderline Personality Disorder Are Finding Help in Various Therapies, Brain Research," *Newsday*, March 6, 2007. The article explains how dialectical behavior therapy is helping borderline patients learn new coping skills and reviews some of the advances in seeking causes for personality disorders.

Web Sites

The Characters (www.eudaemonist.com/biblion/characters). An online version of *The Characters* by the Greek teacher and philosopher Theophrastus is available at this Web site. Theophrastus was probably the first writer to recognize the symptoms of personality disorders in the citizens he encountered in ancient Athens.

Diagnostic and Statistical Manual of Mental Disorders
(http://allpsych.com/disorders/personality/index.html). Students can read an online version of the American Psychiatric Association's *Diagnostic and Statistical Manual of Mental Disorders'* chapter on personality disorders at this Web site.

John W. Hinckley (www.law.umkc.edu/faculty/projects/ftrials/hinckley/HBIO.HTM). John W. Hinckley, who attempted to assassinate President Ronald Reagan, was diagnosed with a schizotypal personality disorder. The University of Missouri, Kansas City, School of Law has made a biography of Hinckley available at this Web site, highlighting his delusional fantasies and obsession with actress Jodie Foster.

Mayo Clinic (www.mayoclinic.com/health/personality-disorders/DS00562). Based in Rochester, Minnesota, the Mayo Clinic is one of the nation's premier research hospitals. The institution has provided an overview of personality disorders on this Web site, including information on symptoms, causes, and the effectiveness of antidepressant drugs.

Index

Picture Credits

About the Author

Hal Marcovitz has written more than one hundred books for young readers. His other titles in the Diseases and Disorders series are *Blindness*, *Infectious Mononucleosis*, and *Brain Trauma*. A former newspaper reporter, he lives in Chalfont, Pennsylvania, with his wife, Gail, and daughter Ashley.